George Clementson Greenwell

A Glossary of Terms

Used in the Coal Trade of Northumberland and Durham

George Clementson Greenwell

A Glossary of Terms
Used in the Coal Trade of Northumberland and Durham

ISBN/EAN: 9783337060169

Printed in Europe, USA, Canada, Australia, Japan

Cover: Foto ©ninafisch / pixelio.de

More available books at **www.hansebooks.com**

A GLOSSARY OF TERMS

USED IN THE

COAL TRADE

OF

NORTHUMBERLAND AND DURHAM.

BY

G. C. GREENWELL, F.G.S., M. INST. C.E.,
COLLIERY VIEWER,

Past President of the North of England Institute of Mining and Mechanical Engineers; Past President of the Manchester Geological Society; Author of "A Practical Treatise on Mine Engineering,"
&c., &c.

THIRD EDITION.

BEMROSE & SONS, 23, OLD BAILEY; AND DERBY.

1888.

TO THE

COLLIERY VIEWERS

OF THE NORTH OF ENGLAND,

WHO, WITH THE AUTHOR, HAVE ACHIEVED

A JUBILEE IN THEIR PROFESSION,

THIS BOOK

IS INSCRIBED.

PREFACE.

THE first edition of the "GLOSSARY OF TERMS USED IN THE COAL TRADE OF NORTHUMBERLAND AND DURHAM," was published anonymously in 1849. The number of copies printed was limited, and was soon disposed of. A second edition, which was merely a reprint of the first, followed shortly afterwards; and it also soon became out of print.

The Authorship of the "GLOSSARY" was acknowledged by the writer in his preface to the first edition of "A PRACTICAL TREATISE ON MINE ENGINEERING," which was published in 1855.

It had for some time been in the mind of the Author to publish a third edition of the "GLOSSARY." The appearance recently of a book having exactly the same title, has hastened the re-publication, particularly as it has, without any acknowledgment, and *very largely indeed*, drawn verbatim from the pages of the original.

The present edition has been entirely re-written. The information contained in the first has been extended and added to; the same style has been observed, as it has been the wish of the Author to include in his book the records of how things were 50 *years ago*, and much more.

Duffield, near Derby,
    18*th August*, 1888.

GLOSSARY.

ADDLE, ADLE.—To earn.

ADDLINGS, ADLINGS.—Earnings.

ADIT.—A drift commonly waterlevel, driven into a mine from a hillside, a grove.

A-FORCE.—To hole a board into an adjoining board unintentionally. (See *Pillar*).

AFTER-DAMP.—(See *Choke-damp*).

AGREEMENT.—(See *Bond*).

AIR.—The current of air circulating through and ventilating a mine.

AIR-BOX.—A square wooden tube used to convey air into the face of a single drift, or shaft in sinking. It ought not to be less, if required of considerable length, than one foot square inside, and may be made larger with advantage.

AIRWAY.—A passage along which the current of air travels.

AMAIN.—" Waggons or tubs are said to run amain, if they get by accident over an incline bank head, without the rope being attached; or through the rope becoming detached or broken." (*W. E. Nicholson, Glossary, &c.*)

APPARATUS.—Machinery at the surface for separating the

small coals, skreened out from the round, into nuts and duff. The small coals which have passed through the skreen, are drawn by the winding engine (whilst winding in the shaft) either vertically or up an inclined framing, in a tub called an apparatus tub, which teems itself at the top of the frame; they are then passed over a second skreen, the nuts to the waggons for sale, and the dead small, or duff which falls through the skreen, if of no value, to the waste heap.

ARLES, EARLES.—Earnest money formerly given to men and boys, when hired at the bindings.

"Previous to 1804, a custom of giving two or three guineas per hewer, as binding or bounty money, had crept into the trade: but in 1804, so great were the fears of procuring the necessary supply of men, that from twelve to fourteen guineas per man were given upon the Tyne, and eighteen guineas upon the Wear; and progressive exorbitant bounties were paid to putters, drivers, and irregular workmen. Drink was lavished in the utmost profusion, and every sort of extravagance perpetrated.

"The evil effects of the system of binding-money produced a re-action, so that it was very soon after discontinued; and for many years the only expense has been two shillings to men, and one shilling to boys." (*Dunn, View of the Coal Trade,* 1844.)

Since the pitmen's strike in 1844, the "Arles" have been altogether discontinued.

AVERAGE WEIGHT.—The mean weight of a tub of coals, at a colliery for any fortnight, upon which the hewers' and putters' wages are calculated: a fixed price being paid for a standard weight, anything above which is called overweight or overplus.

The average weight is usually obtained by weighing two tubs in each score: the average tubs being fixed upon by the weighers, whilst they are being drawn in the shaft to the surface. There are generally two weighers, one appointed and paid by the colliery, and the other by the workmen (1849). At the present time each tub is usually weighed, the average weight of a number of empty tubs, being taken from time to time as the tare; each tub is identified by having a token, or tally, which is a piece of stamped tin or leather, attached to it.

BACK.—A diagonal parting in coal; a description of hitch where the strata are not dislocated. At a back there is frequently a glossy parting, and sometimes a little sooty, dirty coal. When, on approaching a back, it is observed to form an acute angle with the thill of the seam, it is called an East back; when it forms an obtuse angle, it is called a West back. Thus the same back will be an East or West back, according to the direction from which it is mined through. As there is rarely anything to indicate a back, and as there is little or no cohesion between its faces, the coal often and unexpectedly falls away and causes accident.

BACK-END.—In working a four or five yard board, an excavation or kirving is made in the bottom part of the coal, half of the width of the board, and as far as the hewer is able to make it with his pick. This is followed by a vertical cutting, equally far in, next to the side of the place. A hole is then drilled near the roof, and fast side of the coal undermined, and in it gunpowder is placed, and the coal blown down. This is called the sump. The remaining half of the place is called the back-end, and is similarly undermined and shot down.

BACK-HEADWAYS.—(See *Headways.*)

BACKING-DEALS.—Deals placed behind cribs, for the support of the walls of a pit, where the stone is bad. They are generally, when only temporarily required, made of 1¼ inch Scotch deals, and are used in sinking, being replaced by walling, after a foundation has been obtained.

BACK-OVERMAN.—A man who has the immediate inspection of the workings and workmen during the back-shift. His wages are about 21s. per week. (1849.)

BACK-SHAFT.—(See *Engine Pit*).

BACK-SHIFT.—The second shift of hewers in each day. It commences four hours after the pit begins to draw coals.

BACK-SKIN.—A large leather covering for the back and shoulders; it is fastened in front with crossed straps; it is used in sinking and shaft work, as a protection from the falling water. Old, but sound, gig aprons make good backskins.

BADGER.—(See *Brat*).

BAFF-END.—A piece of wood, 15 or 18 inches long, 5 or 6 inches broad, and from 1 to 2 inches thick, used for driving behind cribs or tubbing to bring them to their proper position in a pit. A quantity of these are used in sinking, where much tubbing is required to be put in.

BAFF-WEEK.—Every alternate week. The week succeeding the pay week.

BAG OF GAS.—" A cavity found occasionally in fiery seams of coal, containing highly condensed gas; whether in a gaseous or fluid (or solidified) form has not yet been ascertained. On the coal being worked away until it is no longer equal to resist the elastic force of the compressed gas, the gas escapes with a sort of explosion, displacing the coal, filling the adjoining workings, and firing at the first unprotected lights it meets with, after being brought down to the firing point by a due admixture of atmospheric air." (*Buddle, Account of Explosion at Jarrow Colliery.*)

BAIT.—Provision taken by a pitman to his work.

BAIT-POKE.—The bag in which the bait is carried.

BALANCE-WEIGHT.—(See *Staple*).

BALK.—A species of hitch. The roof of the seam coming down into the coal without any corresponding depression of the thill, thus causing a nip. Balks are most frequent when the roof of the coal is a stratum of sandstone or post. Also a piece of strong timber, usually used in rolley-ways or permanent passages to support the roof, each of its ends being supported by a prop, or by being notched into the wall side.

BALN-STONE.—Roof stone.

BAND.—An interstratification of stone or shale with coal.

BANK.—Above ground.

BANK-OUT.—To teem the coals into a heap as they are drawn, instead of into the waggons.

BANKSMAN.—A man who draws the full tubs from the cages at the surface, when wound up by the winding engine, and replaces them with empty ones; he also puts the full tubs to the weighing machine, and thence to the skreens, upon which he teems the coals. It is also his duty to keep an account of the quantity of coals and stones drawn each day. The banksman's wages are about 4s. per day of 12 hours (1849). He is usually paid by the quantity drawn.

BARGAIN-WORK.—Work such as stone or coal drifting, rolley-way making, &c., let by proposal, amongst the workmen at a colliery, to the lowest offer.

BARRIER.—A breadth of coal left against an adjoining royalty for security against casualty arising from water or foul air. Barriers are left of various thicknesses, frequently 20 yards, but varying according to supposed necessity from 10 to 50, or even 100 yards.

BARROWMAN.—A Putter. One who puts the tubs of coals from the working places to the cranes, flats, or stations, whence they are taken by horses or machinery along the main or rolley-ways to the shaft. Before the application of tramways underground, coals used to be conveyed underground on sledges, and afterwards on barrows, whence the name.

The average day's work of a barrowman, who when putting alone, is a young man from 17 to 20 or 21 years of age, is equal, on level road laid with bridge rails, and with tubs having flanched wheels 10 inches in diameter in the trod, to—

1 empty tub = 3 cwt. pushed 8,280 lbs. yards or ·7057 tons pushed 1 mile, or... ... ... 8,346,240 pushed 1 foot.

1 full tub = 10 cwt. pushed 8,280 yards, or 2·3523 tons pushed 1 mile, or... ... ... 27,820,800 pushed 1 foot.

Total days work 3·0580 tons pushed a distance of 1 mile, or 36,167,040 pushed 1 foot.

And taking the friction at 1-65th part on account of the imperfect nature of the way, and the small diameter of the tub wheels, and being also the mean of six experiments, the mean permanent force exercised by the barrowman for 12 hours is equal to 556,416 lbs. raised 1 foot in 12 hours, or 6·44 lbs. raised 2 feet per second, which is equivalent to 7·728 lbs. raised 2 feet per second for 10 hours, or about one-fourth part of the mean relative, or permanent force of a man, as estimated by Mr. Tredgold.

Barrowmen are usually paid from 11d. to 15d. per score of 6 tons, put an average distance of 80 yards with 1d. extra per score for every additional 20 yards (1849). Small ponies were first used for putting about the year 1842, and have since been, and now are, where convenient, largely substituted for putters.

BARROW-WAY.—The way along which the barrowmen put the corves or tubs of coals. It is either laid with tram plates or bridge plates; but the latter are preferable. Twenty-four inches between the rails is a good gauge, being suitable for both barrow-way and horse-road.

BASTARD WHIN.—Very hard post or sandstone, but not so flinty as to be called whin.

BATEWORK.—(See *Short Work*.)

BEANS.—A description of small coals, so called from their size, produced by further skreening the duff.

BEARING, or BEARING-IN DOOR.—(See *Door.*)

BEATER.—An iron rod, used for stemming or tamping a hole, preparatory to blasting (1849), but must not be used upon the first tamping (Mines' Act, 1872). Iron and Steel prohibited (Mines' Act, 1887).

BEAT-HAND.—(Built?) A hand which, from being vesicated or blistered with hard work, has festered.

BECHE (called by the workman Bitch).—(See *Bore.*)

BEETLE.—" A small locomotive engine driven by compressed air, the invention of Messrs. Lishman and Young, and employed on the rolley-ways at Newbottle Collieries." (*Nicholson.*)

BELL CRANK.—A double crank placed between the ends of a shaft.

BELL PIT.—This is a pit sunk where the mine lies very near the surface : it is commenced of small size, and when the coal or mine ground has been bottomed, it is worked away in every direction round the bottom as far as the workman can cast the mineral with his shovel. The general form arrived at is that of a bell, inverted, whence the name.

BEND.—Yorkshire, or engine bend, is a leather used in grathing buckets and clacks with side leathers, or leather jackets : this leather is moderately stout, and is studded with brass or wood muds.

BEND-AWAY.—The order given by the person in charge for the cage to be drawn to bank.

BEND-UP, or BEND-UP A BIT.—An order given by the person in charge to raise the cage slowly, so that it may be instantly stopped on the order " Hold ! " being given.

BIND.—To hire.

BINDING.—Up to 1810, the binding took place on the Saturday nearest to fourteen days previous to October 10th, but after this year until 1844, on the Saturday nearest to fourteen days previous to the 5th April ; the engagement being from October 10th and April 5th respectively for twelve months. Since 1844, the usual agreement has been to hire for one month; either party being at liberty to terminate the engagement at the expiration of a month's notice (1849); the notice at present is usually 14 days.

BLACK-DAMP.—(See *Stythe*).

BLAST.—An explosion of fire-damp extending over a great part of the workings of a colliery; also to blow down stone or coal with gunpowder or other explosive.

BLEED.—Coal is said to bleed when water oozes in drops from its pores.

BLOW-DOWN.—To bring down coal or stone with gunpowder.

BLOWER.—A sudden and violent discharge of gas from the roof, seam of coal, or floor. (See *Bag of Gas*).

BLOWN-OUT SHOT. (See *Standing Bobby*).

BLUE-METAL.—Indurated argillaceous shale, of a blueish purple colour, resembling that of blue slates.

BOARD (WIDE).—An excavation, a pillar in length, and four or five yards in width, usually driven at right angles to the cleavage of the coal; sometimes, however, when the coal is very flaky and works tender, it is advantageous, the coals being produced in better condition, to drive the boards in the direction of the cleat, when they are called headways boards.

BOARD (NARROW).—An excavation of the same length as a wide board, but driven two yards wide.

BOARDWAY'S COURSE.—The direction at right angles to the line of cleavage or cleat of the coal.

BOLL.—A coal measure. The coal boll contains 9676·8 cubic inches, or 34·899 imperial gallons. (*H. Taylor, Esq., Evid. before Select Committee of House of Lords*, 1829).

BOND.—The agreement to hire between coal owners and workmen. Now an obsolete word: the term agreement being substituted.

BORE.—To ascertain the nature of strata, by means of bore-rods and apparatus connected therewith, which consist of—

1st. *Common Rods.*—They are made of the best iron, ⅞ or 1 inch square, in lengths of 3 or 6 feet, with a male screw at one end, and a female screw at the other end of each length, for the purpose of joining them together as required. There are also short pieces of the length of 6, 12, and 18 inches for the purpose of adjustment. The bottom rod of all has a female screw at each end, the chisel being screwed into it. It is called a box-rod. The common rods weigh about 22 lbs. per fathom.

2nd. *Chisels* are made 18 inches in length, and $2\frac{1}{4}$ inches broad at the cutting edge, and tapering upwards to the screw joint, which is a male screw. The chisel weighs $4\frac{1}{2}$ lbs.

3rd. *Wimbles.*—In boring through shales, the borings adhere sufficiently to the chisel to allow them to be drawn out of the hole; that is to say, when the hole is damp enough to work the borings in shale into clay. In a dry hole, or in boring through posts or sandstones the case is different, and another implement is required to be introduced on withdrawing the chisel. It consists of a cylinder, 24 inches long, open at the bottom and also at the top, about 12 inches below the joint; it has also a partial covering at the bottom, like an auger, for the purpose of retaining the core with which it fills when worked round the hole. Wimbles are also used in boring near the surface through clay. Their external diameter must be such as to admit of their following the chisel. A wimble weighs about 12 lbs.

4th. *Sludgers* differ from wimbles in having a clack near the bottom of the cylinder, and are used when a borehole is so wet that the borings would, unless retained by a clack or some such contrivance, be washed out of the cylinder in being drawn to the surface. The sludger is also useful in boring through a seam of coal, in bringing up samples of coal when cut by the chisel.

5th. *Beche.*—An instrument having some resemblance to the extinguisher of a candle; it is 25 inches long, and weighs 6 lbs. The hollow part extends 16 inches up into the tool, and is $1\frac{1}{2}$ inch diameter at the lower end, and tapers to $\frac{5}{8}$ inch at the upper. It is used for the purpose of extracting the bottom portion of a broken set of rods from the hole.

6th. *Rounder*, resembles a beche externally. It is, however, solid and well steeled at the bottom, and is used for breaking or cutting off any projection which may have occurred in the hole.

7th. *Bracehead.*—A piece of tough ash or oak, 36 inches long, passed through an eye in a short piece of iron, at the other end of which is a male screw to connect with the rods. There are both single and double braceheads; in this case there are two eyes; with the former, two men, and with the latter, four men may be applied; and without other assistance a borehole may be put down 20 fathoms. For a greater depth—

8th. A *Brake* becomes necessary. It consists of a lever from 8 to 12 feet long ; the axis or fulcrum being placed 18 inches or 2 feet from the end above the borehole. To this end a hook is fixed upon which the rods are suspended by a chain attached to a piece of doubled rope which is passed under a bracehead screwed into the top of the rods. When all is ready the lever is weighed down by one or more men, according to the depth of the hole and weight of the rods, which occasions the rods to be raised ; they are then allowed to drop freely back into the hole, the chisel cutting the stratum as it descends. The master of the shift of borers is stationed at the bracehead, by means of which he moves the rods a little in a forward direction at each stroke, so as to keep the hole perfectly circular. He can also distinguish by the touch the nature of the stratum through which the chisel is passing. The rods should be drawn, and the hole cleaned every 6 inches. There are besides other tools such as keys, &c., which are constantly required for unscrewing the rods, when drawing or lowering, and small braceheads called topits to which to attach the rope by a runner, for drawing the rods by means of a jack roll. They are drawn by a rope and block, or set of blocks suspended from a triangle or set of shear legs, placed over the hole. The triangle should not for a deep hole be less than 35 or 40 feet high. In a deep hole it is desirable that the rods should be changed in long lengths; and it is therefore very advantageous to have the top of the borehole lowered a few fathoms by means of a staple. The cost of boring increases with great depth at a very rapid rate, and, as an experienced borer once reminded me, "a few fathoms at the top means a few fathoms at the bottom."

Boreholes are necessary in the faces of drifts in coal or stone for the purpose of exploration in approaching old workings; those straightforward are called front, and those at an angle, flank-holes.

BOTTOM-BOARD.—The bottom of a waggon or truck, which is unfastened when the waggon is required to be discharged into a vessel, or deposit underneath by knocking off a catch.

BOTTOM-ROD.—An iron rod attached at one end to the bottom of the pumping spears, and at the other by an offtake joint to the bucket sword.

BOWK.—A report made by the cracking of the strata owing to the extraction of the coal beneath. (See *Thud*.) Also the noise made by the escape of gas under pressure.

BOX-ROD.—(See *Bore*.)

BRACE-HEAD.—(See *Bore*.)

BRAKE.—(See *Bore*.) Also a band of iron, sometimes faced with wood or flat hemp rope, caused by a lever to press upon a sheave or wheel to check its motion; also a wooden breast applied to the wheel of a waggon or truck, by means of a lever.

BRAKESMAN.—The engineman who attends to the winding engine.

BRANCHES.—The sidings required at a colliery for the convenient separation and loading into waggons of the various descriptions of coal produced; also for the marshalling of trains of waggons, and for other purposes.

BRASSES.—Iron pyrites (sulphide of iron) found in coal; they require careful extraction; they often explode in the fire with a loud report; they can be utilized for the manufacture of copperas. Copper pyrites (sulphide of copper) is occasionally, but rarely, found in coal; it is yellower in colour, and can be scratched with a knife.

BRAT.—A thin stratum of a coarse mixture of coal and carbonate of lime or pyrites, frequently found lying at the roof of a seam of coal.

BRATTICE.—" A partition, generally of deal, placed in a pit, or in a drift, or other working of a colliery for the purpose of ventilation. The former is called a shaft brattice; the latter, the drift, headways, board, &c., brattice, according to the situation in which it is placed. Its use is, to divide the place in which it is fixed into two avenues, the current of air entering by the one, and returning by the other." (*Buddle: First Report of the Society for preventing accidents in Coal Mines*).

Shaft or main brattice is usually made of 11 in. by 3 in. Memel plank; the joints being so dressed that the planks placed edgeways upon each other, may be perfectly close together, and as nearly as possible air tight. There should also be a dowell, or iron bolt, 6 inches long, and $\frac{3}{4}$ inch diameter, for every five feet in length of the brattice planks, passing 3 inches into the adjoining planks for the purpose of stiffening the whole.

Common brattice is made of $9\frac{1}{2}$ inch American deal, cut up into sheets, or leaves, of a size convenient for the height of the seam for which it is required, battened at the back. It is nailed to props set for the purpose (called brattice props), when the roof does not require propping; but if it does, the ordinary timber will do.

Brattice cloth is now, and has for some years, been most generally used for underground work instead of brattice deals. It consists of strong canvas coated with or steeped in tar or other substance to keep it air-tight. (See *Stopping*).

BREAKER.—In working against a goaf there is usually at the distance of a few feet from it, a crack and slight settlement of the roof which has received the above name.

BRIDGE RAILS.—Malleable iron rails, the upper part of which is hollow, with flanches on each side at the bottom, and weighing about $5\frac{1}{2}$ lbs. per foot. They are now much used in barrow-ways instead of tram-plates; the tubs being fitted with flanched wheels (1849). Steel is now very generally used for this purpose.

BROKEN.—Pillar working. The partial working of pillars in fiery collieries was commenced in the Tyne collieries below Bridge, in 1795, the first experiment being made by Mr. Thomas Barnes, in the High Main Seam, in 1795. Before this plan was adopted, only 40 per cent. of the coal could be obtained under a depth of 100 fathoms, 60 per cent. being lost in pillars. After its adoption, 55 per cent. was obtained and 45 per cent. was lost. (*Buddle, Evidence before Select Committee of House of Lords*, 1829).

The process was called "robbing the pillars." Further improvements were made by Mr. Buddle, at Percy Main colliery in 1810, by which from 80 to 90 per cent. were obtained, but an increased quantity of small coals made. (*Buddle*). During the present time, very little coal need, by proper management, be lost in pillar working. No rule can be laid down as to how pillars should be taken off; so much depending upon situation and the nature of the roof, and thill, and coal. The principal thing to be attended to is getting the pillars as quickly off as possible, and to be very careful in getting all the coal practicable, together with all timber, so as by enabling the roof to fall freely, to remove pressure from adjoining pillars, and avoid creep.

BROW.—"The face or escarpment of a trouble or dyke in a coal mine." (Brockett, *Glossary of North Country Words*, 1846.) The front of the depressed roof at a dip hitch.

BUCKET.—"The part of a pump supplied with a fall or lid; as the bucket descends the water rushes through the fall (the column being supported by the clack below), and on the bucket being raised, the fall drops and retains the water which is brought up and" (eventually) "delivered into the landry box." (*Nicholson.*)

BUCKET DOOR PIECE.—The portion of a set of pumps immediately above the working barrel, having a removable door through which the bucket is changed; the bucket door is secured to the bucket door piece by bolts.

BUCKET SWORD.—An iron rod secured to the bucket by being passed through it and cottered; its upper end being connected with the bottom rod of the spears by an off-take joint.

BULL.—To bull a drill hole, consists in filling the hole when in wet stone with strong clay, and then driving a round iron rod with an eye at one end for the purpose of extraction (called a bull), and nearly the size of the hole, to its far end, previous to putting in the powder; the object being to keep back the water from oozing out of the sides of the hole, which by wetting the powder, would prevent it from exploding. Also a carriage attached to the front of a set of tubs descending an underground inclined plane, which supports a movable fork so balanced as to strike into the roof in case of the breaking of the rope.

BUNTONS.—Transverse pieces of wood placed in shafts to which the guides for the cages are attached. (See *Standing Set.*)

CABIN.—An underground office, usually near the shaft bottom, where the overman gives directions as to the apportionment and conduct of the day's work; candles given to the drivers; reports received as to the state of the colliery. (See *Lamp-Cabin*.)

CAGE.—A frame of iron which works between slides in a shaft, and in which since the substitution of tubs for corves, the tubs of coals are drawn to bank, and all passage in the shaft carried on; it is attached to the chain at the bottom of the winding rope by four or sometimes six chains, 8 or 10 feet long.

CALLING COURSE.—The time at which the caller calls from house to house to awake the fore shift men, and afterwards the lads and others; in former times he used to knock at each door and tell the inmate to "waken up and go to work, in the name of God!"

CANCH.—Stone necessary to be taken up or down on account of a rise or dip hitch, or to make necessary tub or horse height.

CALDRON-BOTTOM.—The fossil root of a tree or fern lying on the roof of a seam of coal. It has little adhesion to the overlying stratum, which, where these are present, is usually shale; its presence is difficult to detect, and it drops, often without giving any warning, occasioning accidents which are frequently fatal. It derives its name from the resemblance to the bottom of a caldron or pot; in Somersetshire, it is called with greater propriety a bell-mould.

CANDLES.—"The common pit candles vary in size, but those generally used are forty-five to the pound; the wick is of cotton, and the candle made of sheep or ox tallow, but clean ox tallow is the best."—(*Buddle, Report*). They are not used so small now, the size being from 20 to 30 to the pound.

CANNEL COAL.—A fine compact description of coal, with a conchoidal fracture; it burns with a bright flame, like a candle, whence possibly its name. Its composition is as follows. (*Richardson, Transactions Natural History Society, Newcastle,* 1837).

	LANCASHIRE.			EDINBURGH.	
CARBON	83·789	83·698	83 808	67·434	67·760
HYDROGEN	,,	5·677	5·643	5·394	5·416
AZOTE & OXYGEN	,,	8·077	8·001	12·606	12·258
ASHES	2·548	2·548	2·548	14·566	14·566
		100·000	100·000	100·000	100·000

There are some beds of cannel coal in the Newcastle coal-field; and near the roof, and in the middle of a few of the seams, a few inches of cannel frequently occur.

CANTEEN.—A small wooden flat barrel, containing about half a gallon, in which a pitman carries water or coffee with him to his work. A tin bottle is used for the same purpose.

CAP.—The blue "top" on a candle or lamp when it burns in a mixture of fire-damp and air, not in an explosive condition. (See *Show*). Also to put a shackle on a rope.

CARTRIDGE.—(See *Shot*).

CAPHEAD.—A top placed upon an air-box, used in sinking, &c., for the purpose of catching as much air as possible; its front is kept facing the wind by means of a vane.

CASH.—A soft band. Sometimes found separating one stratum from another; when thin, called a cashy parting.

CASTER.—The work of casters was to shovel or "cast" the coals from the keels into the vessels, at the ports in the side of the same for the purpose. Their wages in former times used to be 2s. per day and a pint of beer.

CATBAND.—An iron loop placed on the underside of the centre of a flat corf bow, in which to insert the hook.

CATCHES.—(See *Keeps or Keps*). Also movable checks by which the tubs are secured in the cages.

CATCHPIN.—A strong oak or iron pin fixed over and to the ends of the beam of a pumping engine, which, in the event of a broken spear, by falling on the spring-beams, prevents the damage that would be occasioned to the top or bottom of the cylinder. (See *Spring Beams*.)

CATHEAD.—An ironstone ball.

CAVILS.—Lots. A periodical allotment of working places to the hewers and putters of a colliery, usually made quarterly, each person having assigned to him by lot that place in which he is to work during the ensuing quarter.

CHALDRON.—The Newcastle chaldron is a measure containing 53 cwts. of coal. The content of the chaldron waggon (custom-house measurement) is 217,989 cubic inches; and that of the boll being 9676·8 cubic inches, the chaldron is equal to 22·526 bolls, and not as usually, but erroneously stated, to 24 bolls. The weight of the boll of coals is therefore $\frac{53}{22\cdot526}$ = 2·35284 cwts. The statute London chaldron is to consist of 36 bushels heaped up; each bushel to contain a Winchester bushel and one quart, and to be 19½ inches in diameter externally; and as it has been found, by repeated trials, that 15 London pool chaldrons are equal to 8 Newcastle chaldrons (*Rees's Cyclopedia*), the London chaldron must be equal to 28·266 cwts. The content of a London chaldron has been variously estimated, viz.—

28·266 cwts. *Beaumont's Treatise on the Coal Trade*, 1789.
27·000 cwts. *Dr. Macnab, Letters to Pitt*, 1793.
26·500 cwts. *T. Ismay, Evidence on Coal Trade*, 1800.
27·762 cwts. *W. Dickson, Evidence on the Coal Trade*, 1829.
    (or 11-21 sts. × 53 cwts.)
28·462 cwts. *B. Thompson, Inventions and Improvements* 1847.

Coal is at present, and has for some years been sold by weight only. By the Coal Mines Inspection Act, 1872, it was enacted that the amount of wages should, after August 1st, 1873, where it depends on the amount of mineral gotten, unless the mine is exempted by a Secretary of State, be paid for by the true weight of the mineral gotten.

CHALKING DEAL.—A flat board upon which the craneman or flat-lad apportions and keeps account of the work done by the putters in the district of which he has charge.

CHAIN PUMP.—(See *Rag-wheel Pump.*)

CHANGER AND GRATHER.—A man whose province it is to keep the buckets and clacks in order, and to change them when necessary.

CHASE, OR CHESS, THE ROPES.—After the winding-engine has been standing for some time, to run the cages up and down the shaft to see that all is right before men are allowed to get into the cage.

CHECK-VIEWER.—A viewer employed by the lessor to see that the provisions of the lease are duly observed.

CHECK-WEIGHER.—The weigher employed by the workmen. (See *Average Weight.*)

CHINLEY COALS. (shingly).—Chinley coals are neither round (or large) nor small, but are such as will pass over the skreen and among the best coals.

CHISEL.—(See *Bore.*)

CHOCK.—Used to prevent the escape of tubs or wagons down an incline. It consists of two blocks of hard wood, one of which can either lie across the rail, or between the rails pointing down the bank and turning on an upright pin placed between the rails; the other also working on an upright pin on the outside of the rails. When the chock is in use the latter block is pointed up the bank parallel with the rail, and the former being placed across the rail, rests against it. When the set is required to move, the outside chock is knocked to a side, and the inside one moves down between the rails.

CHOCKS.—Wooden billets, made of hard wood, usually about 2 feet long, 8 inches broad, and 6 inches thick, built up two and two crossways to support the roof: the column is usually set upon a small quantity of small coal, which being easily picked out enables it to be taken down without difficulty.

CHOKE-DAMP.—The following diagram is illustrative of the combustion of fire-damp or carburetted hydrogen, of which the product is choke-damp, called also after-damp.

BEFORE COMBUSTION. Weight.	ELEMENTARY MIXTURE. Atoms.	Weight.	PRODUCTS OF COMBUSTION. Weight.
8 Carburetted hydrogen.	1 Carbon 1 Hydrogen 1 Hydrogen	6 1 1	22 Carbonic acid 9 Steam 9 Steam
144 Atmospheric air	1 Oxygen 1 Oxygen 1 Oxygen 1 Oxygen 8 Nitrogen	8 8 8 8 112	 112 Uncombined nitrogen
152		152	152

(*Williams, Combustion of Coal.*)

This gas, which is the result of an explosion of fire-damp, is most deleterious and causes more deaths than the fire, in the proportion of three to one. (*R. Elliott, Evidence on Accidents in Mines,* 1835.)

CINDER COAL.—Coal deprived of its bitumen by the action of a whin-dyke or slip.

CLACK.—The low valve of a pump; its use is to support the column of water when the bucket is descending.

CLACK-DOOR-PIECE.—The portion of a set of pumps immediately below the working barrel in a lifting set; it has a removable door through which the clack is changed. In a forcing set there are two clacks both placed in the column of pumps, one being below the junction pipe in the H piece, between the bottom of the plunger or ram chamber and the pumps, and the other above it.

CLAGGY.—A seam of coal is said to have a claggy top when it adheres to the roof, and is with difficulty separated: it most frequently occurs when the roof is post or sandstone rock, and is uneven or scabby.

CLAM.—A movable collaring for a pump, consisting of two pieces of wood indented to receive the pump, and screw-bolted together.

CLEAD.—To cover with planks or deals.

CLEADING.—The plank covering of a winding drum; the deal covering of a cylinder of an engine, &c.

CLEAT.—The vertical joints or facings in coal or stone. There are frequently two cleats in coal, at which, when distinct, the coal is broken into rhomboidal fragments. These cleats do not always intersect each other at the same angle: thus the angles in the Brockwell seam, at West Auckland colliery are 100° and 80°; in the Five-quarter seam at Black Boy colliery, 122° 20', and 57° 40'; in the High Main seam at Willington colliery, 103° 24', and 76° 36'; in the Main seam at Broomhill colliery, 109° and 71°, and in the Main coal at Holywell colliery, 140° and 40°. The following directions of cleat are taken from 73 observations:—

TABLE OF DIRECTIONS OF CLEATS IN COAL IN THE NEWCASTLE COAL FIELD (TRUE MERIDIAN).

BETWEEN W. by N. & W.	W. N. W. & W. by N.	N. W. by W. & W. N. W.	N. W. & N. W. by W.	N. W. by N. & N. W.	N. N. W. & N. W. by N.	N. by W. & N. N. W.	N. & N. by W.	N.	BETWEEN N. & N. by E.	N. by E. & N. N. E.	N. N. E. & N. E. by N.	N. E. by N. & N. E.	N. E. & N. E. by E.	N. E. by E. & E. N. E.	E. N. E. & E. by N.	E. by N. & E.
2	7	3	7	18	21	2	1	0	0	0	0	0	3	2	7	

CLEATS.—Pieces of wood fastened to dry spears for the purpose of steadying them, and preventing them from wearing where they pass through the collarings. Cleats are also placed upon wet spears to steady them, and prevent the edges of the spear-plates and spear bolt-heads from injuring the pumps.

CLINCH OR CLINK BOLTS.—Cross bolts under spear bolts to prevent the spears from stripping.

CLINKERS.—A slag formed upon fire-bars by impurity in the coal.

CLIPPERS, CLIPPUS.—The hook used, in sinking, to attach the rope to the corf, when it is required to be sent to the surface or down the pit. It is constructed with a piece of flat iron, connected by a hinge joint with the turned up end of the hook which is also flat. When the corf-bow is placed in the hook, this piece of flat iron is put down and kept in its place by an iron spring attached to the shank of the hook, and which requires to be pressed back before the corf can be liberated. A corruption of Cliffe's hook.

In the ordinary pit hook used when coals were drawn in corves, the catch was connected with the shank of the hook near the top, and pressed by a spring against the turned up point of the hook after the fashion of the spring hook, by which a chain is attached to a watch.

CLOUR.—A small depression of roof into coal, mostly in a post roof.

COAL-PIPE.—The carbonized bark of a fossil plant; also a very thin seam or scare of coal.

COD.—The carriage or bearing of cast iron, bolted to the underside of the tram, which rests upon the journal of the axle, which is kept in its place by an iron strap.

COKE.—Cinders produced by burning coal in close ovens, only sufficient air being admitted to combine with the volatile carbons : or without any admission of air, the volatile carbon being driven off by external heat, condensed and utilized. The flame produced by the first named process is now by means of flues, frequently applied to raising steam, by being passed under boilers, and to other useful purposes.

COLLARING.—A framing usually composed of pieces of

timber crossed placed under the pump joints in a shaft for the purpose of steadying and supporting the set. Also used for steadying the dry spears of pumps in a shaft. Also for steadying underground horizontal spears, &c. (See *Cleats.*)

COLUMN.—The water above the clack in a set of pumps.

COMPASS.—A pit compass or dial, will be found most useful when divided simply into four quadrants reckoning 90° each way from the north and south points marked on the dial. In all careful surveying underground, the tram-plates or other iron or metal way ought to be taken up for at least four yards on each side of the compass : the surveying lamp should be entirely of copper or brass, and no iron should be found on any portion of the dress or in the pockets of the surveyor. It is also advisable to read off the course from the north end of the needle—always to look through the same sights (the low ones are preferable)—and to survey the same colliery always as nearly as possible at the same time of day, the diurnal variation of the needle being far from inconsiderable. The following table shows the diurnal variation taken at different hours of the 27th June, 1759, by Mr. Canton. (*Philosophical Transactions, Vol.* 51.)

	Hrs.	Mins.	Declination West.	Degrees of Fahrs. Therm.
MORNING.	0	18	18° 2'	62°
	6	4	18° 58'	62°
	8	30	18° 55'	65°
	9	2	18° 54'	67°
	10	20	18° 57'	69°
	11	40	19° 4'	68½°
AFTERNOON.	0	50	19° 9'	70°
	1	38	19° 8'	70°
	3	10	19° 8'	68°
	7	20	18° 59'	61°
	9	12	19° 6'	59°
	11	40	18° 51'	57½°

At present the diurnal variation at Greenwich is about 12' in summer, and 7' in winter. The mean position of the needle is at about 10 a.m. and at 6 p.m. throughout the year.

In the year 1657, at London, the variation was *nil*, and in 1819 it had attained its maximum of westing, which was 24° 41′ 42″.

In 1840 the variation at Greenwich 23° 18′ West.
„ 1845 „ „ 22° 57′ „
„ 1850 „ „ 22° 24′ „
„ 1855 „ „ 21° 48′ „
„ 1860 „ „ 21° 14′ „
„ 1865 „ „ 20° 34′ „
„ 1870 „ „ 19° 53′ „
„ 1875 „ „ 19° 21′ „
„ 1880 „ „ 18° 33′ „
„ 1885 „ „ 18° 1′ „
„ 1888 „ „ about 17° 40′ „

The variation for Newcastle is about 1° 50′ greater; that for Derby 1° 10′ greater; and that for Manchester 1° 45′ greater (1881). But these differences would not be quite the same in 1840. (*From Greenwich Observatory.*)

CONDUCTORS.—(See *Slides*.)

CONICAL DRUM.—(See *Rope Roll*.)

CONSIDERATION.—" Compensation paid to hewers for unforeseen difficulties met with in their work and which are not covered by the score price." (*Nicholson.*)

CONVOY.—The brake formerly applied to one of the wheels of a coal wagon. It had one breast, made of wood; the lever was also of wood. Wood wheels were discontinued on the Tanfield way in the year 1794.

COTTERED.—Applied to stone or coal, hard, cross-grained, tough.

CORF.—A basket made of hazel, of the capacity of from 10 to 30 pecks, formerly used for conveying coals from the working places to the surface. Leading corves are small corves, containing about 6 or 8 pecks, used for carrying stones or rubbish to a stow-board. Since the introduction of tubs about 50 years ago the use of corves gradually ceased. The corves were made and kept in repair by contractors, named Corvers, who were paid by the score of coals drawn, according to the circumstances of the colliery as to depth, wetness, upcast, downcast, &c., sixpence to one shilling per score, or from 1d. to 2d. per ton.

COUNTER-BALANCE-WEIGHT. (See *Staple*.)

COUP.—An exchange of cavils. To be valid it must be with the consent of the overman.

COUPLER.—A boy who couples or connects, by means of the coupling chains, the tubs of coal in order to form a set or train.

COURSING.—Conducting the air backwards and forwards through old workings by means of stoppings, properly arranged. Air is usually coursed or shethed "two and two," or "three and three," according to the greater or less quantity of fire-damp discharged; the meaning being that the current in the former case is conducted up two boards and down two, by means of stoppings called sheth-stoppings, placed in every second wall in each headways-course; every alternate line of walls, in which the stoppings are placed, being open either at the top or bottom of the sheth, so as to afford a free passage; that is to say, suppose it to be required to course the air two and two in a panel of twelve boards, and the air to enter at the bottom of the first board, the following sheth stoppings will be required:—one in the second, sixth, and tenth wall in every headways-course, except the highest (or, preferably, the two highest), and one in the fourth and eighth wall in every headways-course, except the lowest (or, preferably, the two lowest). The going headways-course, at the face, is frequently made a part of the course, the stoppings being replaced by doors called sheth doors (1849), but it is far better to conduct the air singly along the face headways-course by means of board-end stoppings, and course the air behind these stoppings, as described above. This, besides saving the expense of the sheth doors, keeps the air at the face in a purer and better state. This mode of ventilation was contrived by Mr. James Spedding, of Workington, 1760. Where the pillars are worked away behind the whole working, which is the most approved plan, there are comparatively no old workings to course, and consequently the above expense is saved. Also, by shortening the run of the air, and consequently the resistance to its motion, a larger quantity is brought into the mine, and the whole placed in a more efficiently ventilated and safer condition.

Cow.—A wooden or iron fork hung loosely upon the last waggon of a set of tubs ascending an inclined plane. Its use is to stick into the floor and stop the set in case of the rope breaking. "It is also used on crabs and gins to take the weight off horses or men when standing." (*Nicholson.*)

Crab.—A species of capstan, worked usually by horses, for the purpose of raising or lowering heavy weights, such as pumps, spears, &c., in a shaft. Ground crabs are used in sinking for lowering the sinking set of pumps as the pit is deepened. The sinking set is collared to two sets of spears, called ground spears; one spear on each side of the set. At the top of each spear is one of a pair of three, five, or seven-fold blocks, called ground blocks, the other being placed near the pit mouth, and the pumps are lowered by means of the ground ropes which pass through these blocks to the ground crabs. These crabs are worked by men and are of very great power. Steam power is now largely applied to main crab work.

Crab-rope.—Hempen or wire round rope used for pump or other heavy work performed by a crab.

Cracket.—A low wooden stool or seat upon which the hewer can sit in performing parts of his work.

Cradle.—A movable stage, supported by a rope, usually the crab rope, used to repair or do work in the shaft. The cradle should be suspended from the rope by not fewer than four chains. In a sinking pit where it is used for putting in tubbing or walling, &c., the cradle is nearly the full size of the shaft when finished. It is furnished with a door when necessary, so as to allow water to be drawn through it. Provision is necessary for ventilation under the cradle. Sometimes a "half-cradle" is used; for work more easily performed, a "flying-cradle," upon which two men can be seated; where one man only is required, a still smaller cradle is used, which may be a piece of oak or elm, 24 inches long, 6 inches broad, and $1\frac{1}{2}$ inch thick, with a piece of rope passed under it and firmly secured, the upper part of the loop being hooked on to the suspending rope.

CRANE.—Used to hoist the corves of coal from the tram and swing them on to the rolley, the coals being put by the barrow-man from the working places to the crane, and drawn thence by horses to the shaft. At the shaft the corves were lifted off the rolleys by the winding engine and drawn to bank. Upon the introduction of tubs, attached to the trams, for the conveyance of coals, they were run on to the rolleys, which were constructed with transverse dish-plates, to keep the tubs in their places on their passage to the shaft, the place where they were put on the rolleys being called a flat. The tubs are now drawn by horses or machinery along the rolley-ways without the intervention of rolleys, and the place where they are taken by the horses from the barrow-man is called a station.

CRANE-MAN.—A lad 16 or 18 years of age, whose business it was to hoist the corves of coals on to the rolleys with the crane. On the introduction of tubs and flats, a younger description of lads was sufficient, say 15 or 16 years of age; these were named flat-lads; a name which at the stations they still retain. Under whatever name, the crane-man or flat-lad proportions the work, or "places the work," or quantity of coals to be put by the barrow-men among them; so that each may know to which places he is to go for coals, and the quantity he has to put from each place.

CREEP.—The rising, or heaving, or lifting up of the floor in the excavations in a seam of coal occasioned by the pillars not having been left sufficient or not having a sufficiently large area to prevent them from being forced into the thill by the superincumbent pressure. The rising up of dough or clay between the hands when pressed upon it, will illustrate this. The softer the thill, the greater the liability to creep. The progressive stages of creep have been well described by Mr. Buddle (*Evidence on Coal Trade*, 1829).—" The first appearance is a little curvature in the bottom of each gallery; that is the first symptom we can perceive; but we can generally hear it before we can perceive it. The next stage is when the pavement begins to open with a crack longitudinally. The next stage is when the crack is completed, and it assumes the shape of a metal ridge. The next is when the metal ridge reaches the roof. The next stage is when the peak of the metal ridge becomes flattened by pressure, and forced into a horizontal position and becomes quite close; just at this moment the coal pillars begin to sustain part of the pressure. The next is when the coal pillars have taken part of the pressure. The last stage is, when it is dead or settled; that is, when the metal ridge, or factitious ridge formed by the sinking of the pillar into the pavement, bears, in common with the pillars of coal on each side, the full pressure, and the coal becomes crushed or cracked, and can be no longer worked, except by a very expensive and dangerous process."

Subsidence of the surface has now taken place.

CREPT PILLARS.—Pillars of coal which have passed through the various stages of creep.

CRIB.—Common cribs are circles of wood usually oak, from 4 to 6 inches square, used, with the backing deals placed behind them, to support the side of a pit when the stone is bad.

A wedging crib is a large crib, made of metal or oak, always used as a foundation for metal tubbing, and most frequently for walling. These cribs, which are from 12 to 14 inches in the bed, and 6 or 7 inches thick, in a large pit, are, when of metal, cast hollow (the hollow part being next to the pit), and weigh about 1 cwt. per running foot. They are set to the centre of the pit by baff ends and spares, a thin sheeting of oak being placed between the joints, and are then wedged from the back till they are perfectly firm and tight.

A ring crib may be made of metal or oak of the same size as a wedging crib. It is open at the top for the purpose of collecting water, which would otherwise fall down the pit. For a few feet above the crib, the side of the shaft is cut gradually to the back part of the channel, so as to allow the water to drain into it. The cutting is also necessary to allow the crib to be wedged. The water is then boxed or piped away from the crib to the standage, or elsewhere if required.

CRIBLE.—To curry favour.

CROOK-YOUR-HOUGH. (See *Hough*.)

CROP.—The basset or outburst to the surface of a seam of coal or other stratum; also to leave a portion of coal at the bottom of a seam in working; also to set out. (See *Set out*.)

CROSS-CUT.—An excavation driven in any direction between headways course and broadways course.

CROSSING.—An air crossing is an arched way of bricks by which one current of air crosses over another current, or the same current, after having traversed its district; it is also called an overgate or overcast. The roof is taken down on the crown of the arch and sloped down each way into the airway, the current in which is to pass over the crossing. The area of the airway upon a crossing should in every case be fully as large as its ordinary dimensions. The best air crossings, as taking up the least room, are made with the top of 3-inch plank, slivered at the joints, or with laths nailed upon the joints at the top side; the whole covered with a coating of lime. They have sometimes, on account of their liability to destruction in cases of explosion, been constructed with the cover to work with a hinge, so as to admit of its rising when exposed to a blast, and again falling to its place. Sometimes the return is taken under instead of over the intake; in this case the crossing is made in the floor, and is then called also an undergate or undercast. This can only be done when there is no liability to the drowning of the air course under the intake airway.

CROWN-TREE.—A plank about 2½ inches thick and 6 or 8 inches broad, used to support the roof in coal workings, each end of the crown tree being supported by a prop. Crown-trees are best made of larch fir, as being most durable. They are also made of Scotch fir. The price may be from 30/- to 35/- per hundred (1849).

CRUSH, OR THRUST.—This occurs when both the roof and floor of a seam of coal are hard, and when the pillars, insufficient for the support of the superincumbent strata, are crushed by their pressure. The coal is much more injured in this way than by creep.

CUBE, OR CUPOLA.—A shaft sunk near to the top of a furnace upcast, and holed into the shaft a few fathoms below the surface, with a wide chimney erected over it, rising 30 or 40 feet above the surface. It relieves the pit top from smoke. Called also a tube.

DADD.—To dash out a small fire of gas, or a small accumulation of gas with a jacket.

DAM.—(See *Frame Dam.*)

DANT.—Soft sooty coal found at backs, and at the leaders of hitches and troubles.

DARG.—A fixed quantity of coal to be worked for a certain price. This word is seldom used in the Newcastle collieries, but is the general term in use about Scremerston. It is equivalent to the hewing or score price of the Newcastle collieries.

DASHING-AIR.—Mixing air and gas together, until by being completely incorporated the mixture ceases to be inflammable. This is done by giving the air after its first union with the firedamp a considerable length of run or course. The quantity of air must be ample for sufficient dilution.

DAVY-LAMP.—A safety-lamp invented by Sir Humphrey Davy in 1815. It consists of an oil cistern of copper, brass, or other material, containing the wick and oil, and covered by a tight-fitting and close topped cylinder of wire-gauze containing 784 apertures to the square inch, within which firedamp may explode and burn, but without communicating flame to the gas outside of the cylinder. The cylinder should not exceed 1½ inch in diameter and may be 8 inches in height. (*Sir Humphrey Davy on the Safety-lamp and on flame, &c.*) The only case in which the Davy lamp is stated to be unsafe, is when exposed to a rapid current of explosive atmosphere, from which it may be up to a certain point protected by a shield.

The first safety lamp was invented by Dr. William Reid Clanny, of Sunderland, in May, 1813, in which the flame of the lamp was insulated, and supplied with air by means of a small pair of bellows. This lamp was first tried in the Harrington Mill Pit, November 20th, 1815. Safety lamps were also contrived by Mr. Brandling, of Newcastle, and Dr. J. Murray, of Edinburgh, but being dependent upon a regular arrangement of the position of gases in the order of their specific gravities, they were not of any practical utility. At about the same time with Sir Humphrey Davy, Mr. George Stephenson, then an engineer at Killingworth Colliery, invented a safety lamp, of which the principle is essentially the same as the Davy. The application was slightly different, the flame of the lamp being surrounded by a cylinder of glass (since surrounded by one of wire-gauze) and the air admitted into the lamp by means of apertures in the ring at the bottom of the cylinder, the burnt air passing through a perforated copper cap covering the top of the glass. The principle upon which both lamps depend, viz., the impassibility of flame through small tubes, was probably discovered simultaneously by both Sir Humphrey Davy and Mr. Stephenson, but the application of wire-gauze must belong exclusively to the former.

Other lamps have also been contrived, viz., Messrs. Upton and Roberts', Martin's, Mueseler's, Clanny's, &c. ; but as the whole of these are to be referred for their safety to the use of small tubes, or wire-gauze, they are, though in some cases possessing great merit, nothing more than modifications of Davy's or Stephenson's lamp (1849).

Many improvements in safety lamps have been made in recent years, greatly increasing their security under difficult and dangerous conditions. It has been found that whereas at a velocity of current of 6 feet per second, the Davy exploded the surrounding gas ; that at 7 feet, 12 feet and 17 feet, the Clanny, Stephenson, and Mueseler lamps as referred to above, did the same. Lamps of modern construction will not explode until they are exposed to a current of from 30 to 40 feet per second. The fullest information on this subject is given in the Report of the Royal Commission on Mines, issued 15th March, 1886.

DAY-HOLE.—An adit or level, driven in at the side of a hill, for the purpose of working the minerals lying within it. Also called a Day-drift, or a Grove; or a drift driven down in the seam from the out-crop.

DAY-SHIFT.—When a pit is worked both night and day it is said to be worked double-shift, the set of men employed during the day being called the day-shift, and that employed at night, the night-shift.

DEAD.—Unventilated.

DECK.—The platform of a cage upon which the tubs stand when being drawn up or lowered down the pit.

DELIVERY-DRIFT.—Water pumped up a shaft is not usually lifted higher than is necessary ; it is delivered into a drift or adit driven from low ground into the shaft. This is called a delivery or off-take drift.

DEPUTIES.—A set of men employed in setting timber for the safety of the workmen ; also in putting in brattice and brattice stoppings. They also draw the props in the workings from places where they are no longer required for further use. Their wages were about 20s. per week in 1849, at present from 25s. to 30s. There cannot be any fixed rule for the number of deputies to be employed in a pit, this depending altogether upon the nature of the roof and consequent quantity of timber required to bo set for its support, also upon the greater or less quantity of fire-damp produced by the coal. Upon an average the number of deputies may be stated at 1 for every 7 or 8 scores of 6 tons each.

DIAGONAL-STAPLE.—A staple sunk diagonally in the line of the back end of the main beam of a pumping engine and a point in the pumping shaft from 10 to 20 fathoms from the surface. Its use is to divide the work of a double-acting engine between the two ends of the beam, by means of a lever beam in the shaft, placed in a hole or chamber made for the purpose, at the bottom of the diagonal staple. The spears working the low set or sets are hung from the lever end, and are also connected by the diagonal spears passing through the diagonal staple from the same point to the inner end of the beam. The upper sets are attached to the outer end of the beam. The result of this arrangement is that when the inner end of the beam ascends it draws up the diagonal spear, lever or V-bob (as it is called), and low set of spears, the outer end of the beam and high set of spears descending, and *vice-versâ*. (See *V-bob*.)

DILLY.—An inclined plane underground, worked by a balance weight placed upon a tram upon a separate tramway, heavy enough to draw up an empty tub, but lighter than, and drawn up by, a full tub. It is controlled by a brake, so that the ascending empty tub can be stopped and exchanged for a full one at any place upon the plane where required.

DIP.—Declivity of the strata or coal seams; to the dip, below the level.

DIPPER.—A hitch which throws down the coal in front of the drift approaching it. The same hitch approached from the opposite direction would be called a *riser*.

DIRT.—A term to express foulness or fire damp.

DOGS.—(See *Keps.*)

DOOR.—Doors are used underground, where unless a passage were required from time to time, stoppings would be necessary. They are usually placed in pairs sufficiently distant to allow the set of tubs to stand or pass through them without both doors being open at once. Several different descriptions of doors are employed, of which are the following:—

Frame Doors.—A frame door is set in a proper frame made for the purpose. It only opens in one direction, viz., against the current of air, and should always be hung so as to fall to, should anyone passing through it neglect to draw it close. Frame doors are always placed in rolley-ways. They should be 6 feet in height and 5 feet in width. The stanchions or frames should be built up with bricks. Frame doors, placed in the barrow way, should be similarly set, and of sufficient size to allow of the passage of the tubs. The trapper is provided with a place to sit or stand in on the windward side of the door, which he pulls open by means of a cord when required. Man doors, which are placed for convenience of communication between different currents of air, are small frame doors which need not be more than 20 inches square, and are secured by screw locks, the keys to which should only be in the possession of the underviewer, overman, or master-wasteman.

Fly or Swing Doors.—These are set in proper frames, and are so constructed as to open both ways, but so, also, as always to fall close when left alone, with sufficient weight to resist the pressure of the air. They are usually protected by a spring on each side to prevent them from being damaged by the tubs when pushed through them. By having a piece of upright board, 8 or 10 inches broad, nailed on the face of the falling stanchion, and by having a piece of brattice-cloth nailed along the bottom, these doors can be made very effective and are very suitable in the workings, but not in the rolley-ways. Hanging sheets made of brattice-cloth are often substituted for fly-doors.

A *Bearing-in or Main Door* is a door which forces the air through an entire district. This should be a frame door and doubled. A *Sheth Door* is placed in a going headway's course, where otherwise a sheth stopping would be necessary. (See *Coursing.*) This may be either a frame or a fly-door as thought proper.

DOUBLE WORKING.—Two hewers working together in a board or wall. An addition of 2d. per yard to the yard price, or 3d. or 4d. per score to the score price in wide boards is frequently made for the inconvenience supposed to be attached to this manner of working. (1849.)

DOWELL.—An iron bolt, sometimes used in putting main brattice together, a portion of the bolt being let into the under-plank, the remainder passing into a hole in the upper. (See *Brattice.*)

DOWNCAST.—The shaft or drift from the surface by which the fresh air passes into the workings. Also a hitch or slip which casts down the seam below the level at which the hitch is found; it is also called a down-throw or dip hitch.

DOWN-THROW.—(See *Downcast.*)

DRAG.—A piece of iron or wood put between the spokes of a tub or waggon-wheel to check its progress where the dip of the way is considerable. When applied to waggons at bank it is always of wood, and of much larger dimensions. Also the resistance which the air meets with in its passage through the workings.

DRAW.—To remove props which are no longer required in the whole by means of a maul, and in the broken by a pout or punch. (See *Maul,* and *Pout* or *Punch.*)

DREDGE SUMP.—A reservoir through which a current of water is made to flow before passing to a pump, in order that any small stones or sludge may be retained by settlement, so as not to fill up or obstruct the water passage into the pump, or wear away the clack or bucket, or gag the same by sticking between the falls and the shell.

DRIFT.—In coal, an exploring place. Usually a pair of

companion drifts are driven simultaneously for ventilation, one being called the fore and the other the back drift. Drifts in stone (called stone drifts) are mostly single. They are driven sometimes for the purpose of exploration, but more frequently because rendered necessary by the occurrence of dislocations in the strata. Stone drifts are often driven for the purpose of cutting other seams of coal, or the same seam at a different level.

DRILL.—A rod of iron, with a chisel end, used in boring a hole in coal or stone in which powder or other explosive is to be placed for blasting. The hammer used in drilling a hole is called a drilling hammer.

DRIVER.—A boy employed in driving the horses on the main roads underground. He is usually 14 or 15 years of age, and his wages are from 13d. to 15d. per day of 12 hours (1849). At present they are from 14d. to 18d. per day of 8 hours.

DROP.—(See *Staith*.)

DROP-STAPLE.—An interior pit, sunk upwards, by which coals from an upper seam, or from the same seam thrown up by a hitch, are lowered in a cage, lifting the cage with an empty tub as it descends. The drum or sheave is governed by a brake.

DRY-SPEARS.—(See *Spears*.)

DUFF.—Small coals, from which, by means of the apparatus, the nuts have been separated. (See *Apparatus*.)

DUMB-DRIFT.—" A drift by which the return air is carried into the upcast shaft without passing over the furnace." (*Nicholson*.)

DYKE.—A fissure in the strata, filled with basalt and detritus from other rocks; sometimes accompanied by a dislocation. Large slips, or hitches, are also called dykes, as the Ninety-fathom dyke, the Tantobie dyke, &c.

EAT-OUT.—This expression is applied when a level coal drift is turned to the dip, in order to take advantage of (or " eat out") a rise hitch.

ENDLESS CHAIN OR ROPE.—(See *Engine Plane.*)

ENGINE BANK.—(See *Incline.*)

ENGINE PIT.—Pumping pit. A pit the whole or a part of which is used for pumping, and on which a pumping engine is placed. At present the word engine is applied indiscriminately, but in its earlier days it was applied only to the pumping-engine, then called a "fire-engine." The subsequently invented machine for winding was called a steam whimsie and afterwards a winding machine, and now generally a winding-engine.

ENGINE PLANE.—Formerly all level main roads or rolley-ways underground were worked by horses, but engine power was introduced about the year 1841 and is now largely used where the planes are long and the traffic considerable. The full tubs are drawn to the shaft, and the empty tubs returned by either the *Tail rope* or the *Endless chain* system.

The *Tail rope* system is that in which the engine has two drums with a sheave at the far end of the plane. If the line is single, the load is drawn to the shaft by one of the drums, and being also attached to the rope of the other drum (which passes round the sheave) it draws that end also to the shaft, where it is ready on the reversal of the engine to draw the empty train or set of tubs towards the face. The rope which hauls out the full tubs is called the main rope and that which hauls back the empties is called the tail rope. The tail rope is thus twice the length of the main rope. Under this system the trains are long and moved quickly, say 8 or 10 miles an hour.

The *Endless rope* or *chain* is moved at a slow rate, say about 2 miles an hour. It is worked in the case of the rope by a clip pulley, and in the case of the chain, with a pulley in which there are webs, with nicks in them to hold the chain as it passes round the pulley. This system requires a double-way. As the full tubs come out, the empties go in at intervals of 10 or 12 yards or more apart, being attached to the rope or chain by a self-acting clip. Where worked as above described, the comparative "costs per ton per mile are for the tail rope 1·879d. ; for the endless rope 2·061d. ; and for the endless chain 1·379d." (*Trans. N. of England Institute of Mining and Mechanical Engineers, vol.* 17.)

ETTLE.—To intend, appoint, arrange.

FACE.—The innermost extremity of a place working into the solid coal or stone.

FACING.—A cleat.

FALL.—A dropping down of the roof. Bucket or clack lids. (See *Bucket.*)

FAST AND OPEN POINTS.—An arrangement at each end of a siding which by means of groves not so deep as the flange on one side, and deeper on the other side of the way, enables the sets, whether going in or outbye, each to keep its own bye-way, without any switch.

FAST-SHOT.—(See *Standing Bobby.*)

FAST-WALL.—A sheth-wall. The wall in which the bearing-up or bearing-down stoppings are placed. (See *Coursing.*)

FAST-JENKING.—(See *Jenking.*)

FAULT.—Any hitch, slip-dyke, or nip, &c., which renders a portion of the seam valueless.

FEEDER.—A spring or runner of water.

FIERY.—A colliery which produces firedamp in dangerous quantity is called fiery.

FIERY-HEAP.—The deposit of rubbish and waste or unsaleable coal which usually takes fire spontaneously.

FIRE-CLAY.—A refractory clay or shale. (See *Sagre Clay.*)

FIRED.—A colliery is said to have fired when an explosion of firedamp has taken place.

FIRE-DAMP.—Light carburetted hydrogen gas. It is found in most coal mines, and is most abundant in the vicinity of slips and dykes. (It has been found in the lead mines of Derbyshire.) It is only explosive when mixed with from 5 to 14 times its bulk of atmospheric air. Its specific gravity is 0·5594. It is fatal to animal life when in a concentrated state, but, when mixed with air, may be respired to a great extent without apparent injury. It may be produced artificially by distilling in a coated glass flask at a red heat, the following mixture:—

        1 part of stick potassa.
        1 part of dried acetate of soda.
        $1\frac{1}{2}$ part of quick-lime.

All rubbed to fine powder and well dried.

FIRE-LAMP.—A round iron cage supported on three legs, or hung by chains, in which a coal fire is maintained for the convenience of the banksmen and skreeners. Also sometimes placed at the bottom of a shaft to produce ventilation in opening out a colliery.

FIRST WORKING.—(See *Whole.*)

FISH.—To catch up a drowned clack by means of a fish-head. (See *Fish-head.*)

FISH-BELLIED.—An early form of railway rail which had its greatest depth half-way between the supporting chairs, the lower edge being elliptically curved between chair and chair. Cast-iron rails were made of this form. Malleable iron rails of the fish-belly pattern manufactured at Bedlington Ironworks under a patent granted to John Birkinshaw and dated December 2, 1820, were used on the Stockton and Darlington Railway at its commencement.

FISH-HEAD.—An instrument used to draw a clack when covered with water and inaccessible by means of the clack door. It is attached to the bottom rod and lowered down through the pumps and past the clack bow, in passing which two shoulders kept out by springs are forced back into the fish-head, after having passed which, the shoulders are pressed out by the springs, and catching under the bow draw the clack to the bucket door or top of the pump.

FISSLE, FISTLE.—To make a crepitant noise or faint crackling. This is heard in early stages of creep.

FITTER.—A coal broker who conducts the sales of coals between the owner of a colliery and the shipper.

FLANCH OR FLANGE.—The crease or raised part or rim of a waggon or tub wheel running on edge rails. Also the projecting rim at the end of pumps by means of bolt-holes through which the length of pumps is bolted together. Before the bolts are put in weizes made of rope, or spun yarn, or of india rubber, or lead are put between the flanges, inside of the bolts. When the weizes are of lead they should be caulked with a flat-edged chisel after being screwed up.

FLANK-HOLE.—(See *Bore*.) Also a hole put in the flank or side of a drift to widen it by putting in a shot.

FLAT.—(See *Crane*.)

FLAT-LAD.—(See *Craneman*.)

FLAT-SHEETS.—Square or oblong sheets of cast-iron about ¾ inch thick which are nailed upon planking at the top or bottom of a pit and form a metal floor for the free moving about of the coal tubs. They are often also used in the workings where roads cross or converge, as at the top and bottom of small inclines, &c.

FLEET.—"Fleet the rope," or "Fleet the crab." The main crab-rope has three or four turns round the main crab and the tail end of the rope is wound up taut on the tail crab, but as the process goes on, the coil upon the main crab rises, and requires adjusting back or lowering from time to time. To do this a scotch or sprag is put in between the rope and the crab-rope sheave at the bottom of the shearlegs, which securely grips the rope at that point. The crabs are then eased and the crab-rope being slightly slacked the coils are lowered down to their proper position. This operation is "fleeting the rope." With a steam crab there is no "fleeting."

FLOOR.—The surface of the stratum immediately underlying the coal.

FLUE.—A horizontal chimney from boilers at a distance

from the upcast shaft. They require constant and careful examination and are frequent causes of accident. Also the return channels by the side of, or through boilers, by which a greater surface is exposed to the heat of the boiler fires.

FLY-DOOR.—(See *Door.*)

FLYING CRADLE.—(See *Cradle.*)

FOAL.—(See *Headsman.*)

FOLLOWING-IN is when one man works after another in the same place. The same consideration attaches to it as to double working.

FOLLOWING-STONE.—(See *Ramble.*)

FORCING-SET.—A description of pump in which the engine lifts a column of dry spears at the bottom of which there is fixed a ram or plunger which works through a stuffing-box or gland into a vertical chamber beneath. When the engine lifts the ram the water follows it into the chamber through the bottom clack. With the descending stroke the ram forces the water up the rising main, in which a little above the cross pipe there is also a clack.

FORE HEADWAYS.—(See *Headways.*)

FORE OVERMAN.—(See *Overman.*)

FORE-SHIFT.—"The first shift of hewers who go down from 2 to 3 hours before the boys." (*Nicholson.*)

FORE-WINNING.—Winning out in front of other workings.

FOTHER.—A measure of coals, being $\frac{1}{3}$ of a chaldron, or $17\frac{2}{3}$ cwt.; a good single horse cart load.

FOUL.—In an inflammable state from fire-damp having accumulated.

FOUL-COAL.—"Bad coal; soft, danty, or hitch coal; unfit for sale." (*Nicholson.*)—(See *Dant.*)

FOX-WEDGE.—A long wedge driven between two other wedges with their thick ends placed in the opposite direction; it is used to bring forward into the pit the lower part of a segment of metal tubbing if when being wedged it should tend to fall backward out of the true line. It is also called a stob and feather, or plug and feather. An application of this principle to wedging coal was made by the writer in 1869. Two pieces of steel, rounded at the back, and tapered in front as above, were pushed to the far end of a 2½ inch drill hole, and a wedge, being the end of a stout bar, was driven between them. The result was satisfactory.

FRAME DAM.—A dam made of wood and of various thickness, say from 3 to 8 feet, according to the pressure and size of the place in which it is required to be placed. A frame dam is formed of balks of fir-wood, placed endways against the pressure, and tapered, but with the top and bottom surfaces parallel, and accurately dressed and numbered. The coal in a drift where it is proposed to place a dam, should be perfectly sound and strong, and should be cut back at each side, and dressed true to the sweep of the circle to which the balks are cut. When the balks of wood are well in their places, the joints are firmly wedged until the whole is perfectly tight. It would add to the security of these dams if 8 or 10 yards of strong ashlar or brick walling with cement were put in behind them, commencing at 5 or 6 yards back from the dam, to notch the stone-work into the coal walls so as to bind the whole together. It is necessary during the erection of the dam to make provision for the passage of the feeder of water and for the workmen wedging the dam on the inside, with plugs to be drawn through on closing, and also for an outset pipe.

Under moderate pressure the balks may, if the dam is only required to be of small size, be placed crossways and laid upon each other, and then wedged; or, they may, for still slighter resistance, be constructed of two rows of 3-inch planks set on edge, and parallel, say 18 inches apart, with good clay or sifted dry soil carefully rammed between the sides. They must be well supported on both sides by good props.

FREE LEVEL.—(See *Adit.*)

FUR, FURRING.—The deposit, usually carbonate of lime,

from limestone or other impregnated water, in pipes, boilers, &c.

FURNACE.—A large fire placed near the bottom of the upcast shaft, which by rarifying the air contained in the upcast shaft, causes that disturbance of equilibrium between its column and a column of cold air of equal length, which occasions a constant current of air to travel to and up the upcast shaft. This current is, by proper arrangements, employed to ventilate the colliery workings. The size of the furnace will, of course, vary with the requirements of the mine in which it is to be placed. Thus a furnace 6 feet in width, which in one seam of coal and for the confined workings of a small colliery, would be ample, would be found quite inadequate to cause an efficient ventilation of extended workings in a fiery seam of coal. A furnace of the width of 10 feet with the bars 6 feet long—the height above the bars to be 5 feet, with the arch elliptical—the area of the furnace drift to the upcast shaft to be not less than 50 square feet, and to rise from the back of the furnace to the shaft at the rate of 1 in 3, the whole being well attended to, will in most cases be sufficient. In a very extensive colliery where much ventilation is necessary, two or even three such furnaces are applied.

FURTHERANCE.—4d. per score paid in addition to the putting price to hewers for putting. (1849.)

FUZE.—Used in blasting as a substitute for a "kitty." It consists of a waterproof flexible tube about the size of the shank of a clay tobacco pipe, with a fine core of gunpowder or other composition. It is placed in the cartridge and stemmed with it in the shot-hole. It affords, after being ignited, ample time for safe retirement before the explosion takes place. It is frequently ignited by electricity. (See *Kitty* : *Match*).

GAG.—An obstruction in the falls or lids of a bucket or clack which prevents them from working. (See *Dredge Sump*).

GALLOWS TIMBER.—A crown-tree with a prop placed under each end.

GANISTER OR GANNISTER.—A very hard and siliceous fire-clay found beneath some of the seams of the lower coal measures. It contains stigmaria roots. It is manufactured into fire-bricks of a highly refractory character, which can be imitated by grinding and mixing up fire-stone post with a less refractory clay. This post is also called ganister.

GAS.—Usually carburetted hydrogen is referred to. Occasionally sulphuretted hydrogen has been found in old wastes. This is easily detected, where present, by its smell. Carbonic acid gas, or stythe, is frequently found in great abundance in coal mines, especially where the seams worked are found at moderate depths from the surface; and a pernicious gas has been occasionally found to issue from old wastes which is fatal to animal life, but in which a candle will continue to burn with undiminished brilliancy. This has been considered to be owing to a mixture of sulphuretted hydrogen with atmospheric air, 1-50th part of which may produce a compound possessing the above properties; but as in a case which occurred at Hartley Colliery, the smell of sulphuretted gas was not described as being present where the man was found dead by the side of his burning candle, the inference is that death was caused by some other gas, most probably by carbonic oxide. The author has knowledge of an instance of the existence in considerable quantity of sulphuretted hydrogen in the Top Hard (Barnsley) seam of coal in South-Yorkshire, and also of "white-damp" or carbonic oxide, in the White Ironstone Mine in Glamorganshire. "White-damp" is well known in South Staffordshire, but it is there no doubt the result of the spontaneous combustion or gob-fire, which is always more or less prevalent.

GATEWAY.—"A passage through the goaf secured by a pack-wall on each side, for the purpose of bringing out the coals worked on the long-wall system." (*Nicholson.*)

GEARS, PAIR OF.—(See *Gallows-timber.*)

GEORDY.—The safety-lamp invented by George Stephenson. (See *Davy*.)

GIN.—An apparatus consisting of a drum fixed upon a vertical shaft, to which a lever, called a "start" is attached. A horse yoked to the end of the lever, and moving in a circular track, causes the drum to revolve, and to wind or unwind a single rope, or to wind and unwind a pair of ropes working over pulleys into a pit, or where required. Gins are constructed with the barrel or drum from 3 or 4 to 15 or 18 feet diameter. Large-sized ones are usually worked by two horses, yoked abreast. Before the application of the steam-whimsie to drawing coals, gins, called also whims, or whim-gins, were used for the purpose.

GIRDLE.—When a stratum of blue or grey metal has interspersed with it bands of post, without partings so as to separate them into complete strata, it is said to be blue or grey metal with post girdles.

GOAF.—A space from which the coal pillars have been extracted. It is usually in the first instance a large dome, resting as the extent increases upon the wreck which has fallen from the roof of the exhausted space. Eventually the pressure to a large extent re-consolidates the whole, the surface subsiding.

GOB-FIRE.—Spontaneous combustion in a goaf. Very rare in the North of England.

GOING-BOARD.—When the crane, flat, or station, is not at the end of the headways-course at the face, and the coals are brought down to it by a board for one, two, or more pillars, this board is called the going (or "gannen") board.

GOING-HEADWAYS.—Usually the headways-course next the face.

GOWK.—(See *Rider*.)

GRATHE.—To put in order, to dress; to replace a worn clack or bucket leather.

GRATHELY, GRADELY. Trim, tidy.

GREASER.—A boy who greases the tub axles at bank. A machine, in passing over which the axles are greased automatically.

GREY-METAL.—A slightly siliceous indurated clay of a light grey colour.

GREY-METAL-STONE.—Grey metal very siliceous and gritty.

GREY-POST.—Sandstone of a grey colour.

GROUND-CRAB.—(See *Crab.*)

GROUND-ROPES.—(See *Crab.*)

GROUND-SPEARS.—(See *Crab.*)

GROVE.—A drift or adit driven into a hillside from which coal is worked. A drift into a seam of coal from the outcrop.

GUIDES.—(See *Slides.*)

GULLETS.—Vertical cracks more or less open. Mostly confined to beds of post, sandstone, or rock. At and near the outcrop of such beds, rainfall or other water passes rapidly into mines beneath.

HACK.—A heavy and obtuse pointed pick of the length of 18 inches and weight of 7lbs. used in sinking or stone work.

HADE.—The slope or inclination of the leader of a slip-dyke.

HALF-BALK.—(See *Balk.*) A balk sawn down the middle into halves. Used where the roof is not so heavy as to need a balk.

HALF-MARROW.—(See *Headsman.*)

HALF-WORK OR HALF-WARK.—When the day's work is half over, or when by reason of bad trade, half-time is worked.

HAND-FILL.—To separate the small from the large coals in the mine, the latter being filled by the hand into the tub or corf, and the former thrown to the side of the working place, or filled separately as required.

HANG.—To incline or dip.

HANGER-ON.—(See *Onsetter.*)

HANGING-ON.—The occupation of the onsetter, also the place where tubs are put into the cage.

HAUD-OFF, HOLD-OFF.—Keep back. Called by a barrow-man putting a full tub or corf to another meeting him with an empty one, the latter being obliged to get out of the way.

HEADSMAN.—A lad not strong enough to put alone, but able to do so with the assistance of a little boy, who performs his part by pulling the tub by a couple of ropes or traces attached thereto, called soams. The little boy is called a foal. He sometimes assists the headsman by pushing behind the tub beside him. The wages made by the headsman, who is 16 or 17 years of age, are about 2s. 9d. per day of 12 hours, the foal being paid 1s. to 14d. per day (1849). When the boys are of the same age or strength they are equally paid and are called half-marrows.

HEAD-TREE.—A piece of a crown-tree, a foot long, placed upon a prop to support the roof, the head-tree being to extend the bearings of the prop.

HEADWAYS.—The direction of the cleat, also a place or holing driven in this direction. When a pair of headways are driven for exploring or winning the coal, they are called exploring or winning headways, the principal of which is called the fore-headways, and the other the back-headways.

HEADWAYS-COURSE.—A line of walls or holings extending from side to side of a panel of boards.

HEAPSTEAD.—The elevated frame work of wood or iron at bank, to the top of which the pit is continued above the surface, to provide the necessary height to pass the coals over the skeens into the waggons.

HEAVE.—(See *Creep.*) Also to heave the crab, raising the load.

HELPER-UP.—A lad employed to assist the barrow-man out of a dip place.

HEWER.—A man who works coals. His age ranges from 21 to 70. His usual wages (1849) are from 3s. 9d. to 4s. 3d. per day of 8 hours working, and his average employment 4 or 5 days in the week. He also has, as part of his wages, a house containing two or three rooms, according to the number in his family, and a garden, of which the average size may be 6 or 8 perches; also a fother of small coals each fortnight, for the leading of which he pays sixpence.

HEWING-DOUBLE.—(See *Double-working*.)

HITCH.—An abrupt elevation or depression of the strata to the extent of from a few inches to the thickness of the working seam of coal. When of larger dimensions it is called a slip or slip-dyke. Adjoining to a hitch or slip the coal is often inferior, and near to very large slip-dykes there is frequent evidence of the existence of great heat.

HOGGER.—A wide leather pipe used to deliver water into a cistern.

HOGGER-PUMP.—The top pump of a set, with a short delivery pipe cast into it at right angles, near the top. The hogger is lashed on the short pipe.

HOGGERS.—Stockings without feet, chiefly used by the barrow-men or putters.

HOLING.—The communication between a pair of places.

HOLING-ABOUT.—When the coal has been won the first operation is to get an air current between the down-cast and up-cast shafts, and to form off the shaft pillars or walls. As these are sometimes of very large dimensions, and as the coal when first tapped is liable to discharge fire-damp very freely, and as it involves driving considerable distances with bratticed air, very great care is necessary. This operation is called "Holing-about." It was in holing-about in the Bensham seam at Wallsend Colliery that 52 lives were lost on the 23rd October, 1821.

HOOKER-ON.—(See *Hanger-on*) The hooker-on used before the introduction of guides, to strike the hook, or hooks, at the bottom of the pit, on to the corf bows.

HORNY TRAM.—(See *Tram*.)

HORSE BACK.—A small balk or depression of the roof. (See *Balk*.)

HOUGH.—" The posterior part of the knee joint."—" The ancle bones more or less completely united." (*Webster's Dictionary*.)—According to Brockett, hoff or hock is the thigh.

"Crook your hough!" the friendly salutation of a pitman who wants you to sit down and "have a crack" scarcely allows hough to have this meaning. It means either to sit on a seat, or on your hunkers; originally, in all probability, the latter.

HOVEN.—Crept. (See *Creep*.)

HOVER.—" Hover a bit."—To pause and consider before action.

" How!" To which the reply is " How AGAIN!" The salutation and response of two pitmen, near to or within hail of each other. It may be friendly or otherwise, but is usually the former.

HOWDIE.—A midwife.

HUDDOCK, HUDDICK. —The cabin of a keel.

HUNKERS.—Sitting on the hunkers. Sitting with the balls of the feet upon the ground and the knees bent, so that the thighs rest on the calves of the legs. This position no doubt became habitual to pitmen from the nature of their underground work, and the conditions under which it is performed.

JACK.—During sinking, whilst the two pits or a pit and a staple are being sunk simultaneously by means of two gins, one of them, to prevent mistakes, is usually called a jack.

JACK HEAD.—(See *Staple*.)

JACK-ROLL—A winch used for sinking moderate depths, both underground and at bank. Called in West Durham, " Row and Stoches." (Roll and Stanchious?)

JACKANAPES.—A succession of frames with pulleys or sheaves suspended therefrom to carry an overhead rope.

JENKING.—A fast jenking is a narrow place driven lengthways in a pillar of coal, but unholed into the board on either side of the pillar. A loose jenking is a similar place driven along the side of the pillar and open to the board along that side. These places are mostly driven in working pillars. Wherever practicable, when a jenking is necessary, it should be driven loose sided, a fast jenking very frequently causing a creeping to take place, and almost invariably rendering the pillar or wall in which it is driven crushed and useless, although to this there are exceptions.

JET.—A species of coarse cannel coal, nearly approaching to a black stone. It burns with a bright flame, but loses little bulk in the fire. Some of these black-stones or shales contain upwards of 20 gallons of oil to the ton.

IN-BYE.—In the workings, or away from the shaft.

IN-BYE SIDE.—One place further into the workings than another, is said to be on the in-bye side of it.

INCLINE, INCLINED PLANE.—If one end of a plane is higher than the other it forms an incline or inclined plane. If coals are required to be brought down it, and the inclination is sufficient to enable the descending load of full waggons or tubs to take up the empty set without any aid but that of gravitation, the way is made into a self-acting inclined plane. If coals are required to be brought up the incline, engine power is necessary.

An underground self-acting plane should not have a less inclination than $1\frac{1}{4}$ inch to the yard, 1 inch being barely sufficient to cause motion. According to Mr. B. Thompson, 8 loaded chaldron waggons descending a plane of $\frac{5}{8}$ of an inch per yard will bring up 8 empty ones at a good working speed. 6 loaded waggons require a fall of $\frac{3}{4}$ inch to the yard, and 4 loaded waggons require $\frac{7}{8}$ in. to the yard. (*Inventions, Improvements, and Practice.*)

INSENSE.—This word means more than to explain. It means making the person to whom the explanation is given thoroughly understand such explanation.

INSPECTOR.—A man employed at the surface to attend to the cleaning and skreening of the coals. His wages are usually 3s. per day, or 18s. per week, with his house and firing free. (1849.)

An underground inspector is required to attend to the working of the coals, and to see that proper pains are taken to make them large and good. He is also required to attend to the straight driving or holing of the places, and to set on compass marks for the purpose. The back over-man, where a colliery is not overcharged with fire-damp, and his time and attention not sufficiently engaged in attending to the safety of the mine, performs the above duties during his shift. The wages of an inspector are 21s. or 22s. per week, with house and firing free. (1849.)

INSTROKE.—In many leases of coal it is stipulated that the coal demised is to be worked by means of pits to be sunk upon the property, in which case it is not unusual to allow any adjoining royalty to be worked by means of drifts, properly provided, on payment of a rent for this privilege which is called an *outstroke* rent, the drifts being called *outstroke* drifts. The coal which is so worked is worked by an *instroke*, or, if any portion of the royalty first named is worked by means of drifts from the adjoining royalty, this constitutes an outstroke from the adjoining royalty, but is an instroke into the royalty upon which the pits were sunk, the whole of the coal thus worked being drawn at such pits.

INTAKE.—The airway along which the fresh air is conducted into a place, district, or mine.

JOWL.—A sort of "tattoo," beaten with a hammer, and in response, upon the faces of two places or drifts near holing, or intended to hole into each other, by a person in each place, for the purpose of ascertaining by the sound their relative positions.

JUD.—A portion of the seam kirved, nicked, and ready for blasting, called also 'vantish, 'vantage, or advantage; also a portion of a pillar in course of being worked away in the broken mine.

JUMP.—To drill a hole for blasting with a jumper.

JUMPER.—A drill made of greater length than that commonly used, and having the head swelled out to make it heavy. It is driven by the hewer with both hands. The plan was introduced into the North by South country miners about the year 1832, but has not been much practised.

KEEPER.—(See *Inspector.*)

KEEL.—A vessel used to carry coals from the Staiths above the old bridge on the Tyne, and above the shipping berths on the Wear, to the ships. A keel is a broad flat vessel (on the Tyne sharp at both ends) carrying 8 Newcastle chaldrons or 21 tons 4 cwt.

KEEPS OR KEPS.—Movable frames or supports of iron, which if left free project about $1\frac{1}{2}$ inches into the shaft top at each side, beneath the level of the settle-boards or flat-sheets by the thickness of the bottom of the cage. Their use is to support the cage containing the tubs of coals when drawn to the surface, the cage rising between the keeps and forcing them backwards; but when the cage is drawn above the keeps they fall forward to their places, forming a rest for the cage, until the full tubs are replaced by empty ones. The keeps are then drawn back by the banksman after the cage has been raised, and so held until the empty cage has passed through.

When there is a hanging-on in the shaft, the keeps are weighted so as always to keep back, except when moved forward by the onsetter.

KENNER.—An expression signifying that it is time to give up work, shouted or signalled down the shaft by the banksman where practicable, and conveyed into the workings from mouth to mouth or by other signal.

KEY.—(See *Bore.*)

KIBBLE.—A wooden tub, usually square, and of the

capacity of about 20 gallons, used in conveying rubbish from one place to another. It is placed upon a tram. It is frequently made with a bow, similar to a corf-bow in shape. The bow is sometimes hinged. Used in sinking wells, carrying mortar, &c.

KICKUP.—A cradle made of iron placed at the head of each skreen, and supported by a short journal at each side, each bearing being supported by a metal stanchion. It is so balanced that when a full tub of coals is run into it, the cradle with the tub turns over, and the coals are discharged upon the skreen, this position being maintained by a brake until the tub is emptied; on easing the brake, the empty tub is returned on the cradle to its horizontal position, and taken back to the shaft.

KINK.—To curl into a kind of knot, as highly-twisted rope, especially wire rope, does.

KIRVING.—A wedge-shaped excavation, made by the hewer with his pick, at the lower part of the seam preparatory to blasting. A kirving should seldom be less than 36 inches from the front to the back side, nor exceed 16 inches in height at the fore side, in a hard coal; in a soft coal, with a good parting at the bottom, the kirving may be deeper, and the height at the front less. The coals obtained from the kirving are to a large extent small, and as the size of the kirving is pretty constant, and irrespective of the thickness of the seam, it follows that a greater percentage of small is made in working a thin than a thick seam, the hardness of the two seams being similar. It is of great advantage to have at the bottom of the seam a swad, soft enough to prick in, as it enables a considerable quantity of chinley coal to be got out of the kirvings by careful work.

KIST.—A chest. The deputies' kist is used to keep their tools, plate and brattice nails, &c., in.

KITTY.—A piece of straw, about 4 inches long, filled with gunpowder. It is placed in the pricker hole, which is open to the cartridge or *shot* in the drill-hole, and the end of the kitty nearest to the cartridge being closed and the outer end open, it follows that when a light is applied to the latter, the kitty, after the manner of a miniature rocket, flies along the pricker-hole and ignites the powder.

KNOCK-OFF-HOOK.—A hook at the end of a set of waggons to which the rope is attached, from which, by the withdrawal of a cottrel or the knocking off of a catch, the set can be detached when in motion.

Also a hook by means of which the rope is detached from the cage when it is drawn too high by the winding engine. This hook is so contrived as when the rope is detached to support the cage upon a ring, fixed under the pulleys, through which the hook has passed.

KNOCK-OFF-JOINT.—(See *Off-take joint*.)

LAID-IN.—When a colliery has ceased working from being exhausted, or from any other cause, and is dismantled, it is said to be laid-in.

LAID-OUT.—A laid-out tub of coals is a tub of coals containing stones or foul coal beyond a certain specified quantity, usually one quart, the hewer of such tub being fined according to the amount of such stones, &c., found in the tub.

LAME-SKIRTING.—Taking coal out of the side of an excavation. To make a narrow place wide, or a wide place wider. A term peculiar to the Etherley district. When not ordered to be done, it is a fraudulent way of getting coal with little trouble.

LAMP-CABIN.—A place above ground, or underground near the pit bottom, where the safety-lamps are repaired, cleaned, examined, lighted, and locked, before being handed to the workmen in cases where naked lights are not allowed to be taken from the bottom of the shaft. In other cases the lamps are repaired as above, but naked lights are used until stations are reached, where the lamps are lighted by responsible persons, beyond which stations no naked lights are allowed.

LANDING.—The top or bottom of a self-acting incline, or of an engine bank, or the ends of an engine plane.

LANDRY-BOX.—A wooden box placed at the top of a set of pumps, into which the water is delivered and spouted to where required.

LANDSALE.—Coals sold to carts at a colliery for direct delivery. Also in bags, and taken away on horses' or asses' backs into out-of-the-way places. Also a colliery to which there is no railway, or tramway, or canal, is called "a landsale," or a landsale pit. Of these there are several towards the out-crop of the coal measure and limestone seams of coal.

LAYERED.—Choked up with mud. Commonly applied to the falls of a bucket or clack thus prevented from working, or to the choking of the snoreholes of the windbore, when the waterway through them is impeded.

LAZY-BALK.—" A balk of timber placed at the top of a skreen or hopper, against which the top of the tub is thrown in teeming to prevent the tub going over, where there is no cradle or kickup." *(Nicholson.)*

LEADER.—The gut of a hitch or slip-dyke.

LEASE.—A formal agreement, for a term of years, between the proprietor of a royalty and an adventurer or adventurers who work the mine. Leases are for various terms, usually from 21 to 63 years, and generally with powers on the part of the lessees to relinquish at the end of any year, or third year, on giving 12 months' previous notice. " Leases under the Dean and Chapter of Durham were formerly granted for original terms of 21 years, renewable every 7 years on payment of a fine, or on a certain annual rent and tentale rent, and sometimes on the payment of a fine and tentale also, in which case the fine covered a stipulated number of tens, to be worked annually. Leases under the Bishop of Durham were generally for three lives, and some (but few) for years under reserved annual rents, and renewable by fine in both cases." *(Buddle, Evidence before Select Committee of House of Commons, 1838.)* The fine for renewal of Dean and Chapter leases was about $1\frac{1}{2}$ years' purchase of the estimated rental of what the mine was worth to let. New leases of church mines are granted by the Ecclesiastical Commissioners.

LED.—A led tub or corf means a spare one, for the barrowman to leave empty with the hewer whilst the full one is being put to the flat, the empty one being filled by the hewer against the return of the barrowman with another empty one.

LEVEL.—A drain cut in the bottom stone to set away or convey water. A pair of levels is a pair of drifts, driven in the water level direction of the strata for the purpose of winning coal.

LEVEL-FREE.—Drained by means of an adit or free-level.

LIFT.—To heave at the bottom, to creep; also a column or parallel columns of pumps; also a broken jud. (See *Jud*).

LIFTING-SET.—A description of pump in which the engine lifts a column of spears (which work in the column of water in the pumps or pipes) at the bottom of which is placed a bucket which works in a chamber called a working barrel. When the engine lifts the bucket, it lifts the whole column of water above it, and at the same time the water below follows the bucket through the clack.

LIG.—To lie down.

LINE.—To survey.

LINING-MARK.—A drill hole in the roof with a wooden plug driven into it to show where the next lining is to commence. The plug is for the purpose of inserting a small fork from which to hang a plumb-line, behind which to hold the candle or lamp which forms the back-sight. The fore-sight is also fixed by a temporary plumb-line suspended from a piece of clay stuck to the roof.

LIP OF SHAFT.—The bottom edge of a shaft circle where open to the seam workings.

LIPPEN.—To reckon or calculate upon.

LOFTING.—Wood, usually old refuse, placed upon the top

of the ordinary balks or crown-trees, used in timbering through a fallen place, for the purpose of keeping up the loose stones, which would otherwise fall between the common timbering. This mode of timbering is practised in close drifting through a heavy fall, which is less expensive than ridding. Lofting is also frequently used when a place is ridded, part of the stones being conveniently stowed upon the timber.

LONG-WORK, OR LONG-WALL, OR LONG-WAY.—A system of work in which the whole of the coal is removed in long face, without any preliminary preparation by pillars, the roads to the face being either supported by pack-walls made from the stone taken down to make road-height or from elsewhere, or by pillars of coal left at either side. This mode of work is of comparatively recent introduction into Northumberland and Durham, due to the necessity of working thinner seams of coal than formerly.

LOOSE ("LOWSE").—Finish working. (See *Kenner, Jenking*).

LOW.—A light.

LOW-ROPE.—A piece of tarry rope, used as a torch. Sometimes used in shaft or pump-work. The rope passing from the under side of the rope-roll or drum, and over the pulley.

LUM.—A chimney placed upon the top of an up-cast pit for the purpose of lengthening it.

MACHINE.—The engine for drawing coals. Winding-engines or machines are usually constructed to work with high pressure steam, but condensing-engines, although in the first instance more expensive, are much cheaper in the end, the repairs of the boilers being comparatively trifling, and the labour in firing and cost of coals less. A ready rule for calculating the power of a high pressure engine, the diameter of the cylinder, and the pressure of steam on the piston being given, is as follows :—

Square the diameter of the cylinder in inches, multiply

by the pressure of steam in lbs. per square inch, and divide the product by 400.

In the case of the condensing-engine, multiply by the sum of the steam and vacuum pressure.

MAIN-CRAB.—(See *Fleet.*)

MAIN-ENGINE.—The pumping-engine, until recently usually a condensing beam-engine. The following is the rule for finding the quantity of water which an engine will pump from a given depth:—

Let H = Horse-power of engine.
F = Depth of pit in fathoms.
G = Quantity of water in gallons per minute.

Then $\dfrac{H \times 550}{F} = G$.

and having any two of the above data given, the third can be found.

MAIN-ROPE.—(See *Engine-plane.*)

MAKINGS.—Small coal made in kirving and nicking.

MAN-DOOR.—(See *Door*).

MAN-HOLES.—(See *Refuge Stalls*).

MARROW.—A partner.

MASTER-SHIFTER.—The person in charge of the shifters. (See *Shifters, Shift.*)

MASTER-WASTEMAN.—The person who has charge of the wastemen. (See *Wasteman, Waste.*)

MATCH.—A small piece of candle end or greased twine or tape placed horizontally beneath the end of the kitty used to ignite the powder in blasting. When everything is ready, the workman applies a light to the point of the match, which he has made of sufficient size, and placed in such a position as in burning to occupy time enough before the flame reaches the kitty to allow him to retire to a safe place. Frequently where lamps are used a wire inserted through the gauze and heated to redness in the flame of the lamp is used to ignite fuse, substituted for the kitty.

MAUL, MELL.—A hammer used in setting props, driving wedges to force down stone or coal, and in drilling in stone to drive in the drill; also, with a long handle, to draw props.

MAVIES.—It may be; perhaps.

MEETINGS.—" Where the cages pass each other in the shaft, or where the full and empty sets pass each other on a self-acting plane." (*Nicholson.*)

METAL.—Shale. (*Plate*, of the lead mining districts.)

METAL RIDGE OR METAL RIG.—(See *Creep.*)

MILLSTONE GRIT.—Hard coarse post with small pebbles of quartz lying immediately at the bottom of the coal measures.

MISTRESS.—An oblong box, wanting the upper part of the front side, and carried upright, having a round hole in the bottom to allow the candle to be raised (as it burns down) through clay to support it, and keep the hole close. The use of the mistress is to carry a lighted candle in a current of air. Used by the drivers.

MONKEY.—A self-acting lever placed between the rails at the top of an inclined plane, the heavy end of the lever being to the dip and the light end rising above the level of the tub axles. On ascending the plane, the axles depress and pass over the light end, which so soon as they have passed is raised again, and prevents any running back of the set. The same object is gained by having a side chock pointing to the rise, and balanced so as to lie diagonally over the rail; it is pressed back by the tubs in passing, and afterwards falls back into its place behind the last wheel of the set.

MOTHERGATE.—The continuation of the rolleyway beyond the flat into the workings. At a future period converted into rolleyway.

MUSHY.—Coal or shale soft and friable, often found near a hitch.

NARROW BOARD.—(See *Board.*)

NARROW-WORK.—Excavations 3 yards in width and under, for which, above the hewing price, an extra price per yard is paid.

NATTLE.—(See *Fissle*.) By nattle is implied a slightly increased action of the creep.

NICK.—To cut the coal vertically, next to the side of the place, similarly to the kirving, preparatory to taking down the jud.

NICKINGS.—The small coals made in nicking.

NIGHT-SHIFT.—(See *Day-shift*.)

NIP.—The effect produced upon the coal pillars by creep; a crush or squeeze. Also an approach of the roof and thill of a seam of coal towards each other, usually of the former towards the latter, the seam having for a greater or less breadth being occasioned almost or even entirely to disappear. Occasioned by denudation.

NOOK ("NEUK").—A corner of a working place at the face; also, the corner of a pillar of coal.

NUTS.—Re-screened small coal. (See *Apparatus*.)

OFF-PUTTERS.—(See *Staith*.)

OFF-TAKE, OFF-TAKE DRIFT.—(See *Delivery drift*.)

ONSETTERS.—Men who put the full tubs in and take the empty tubs out of the cage at the shaft bottom, or at any other landing or stopping place. They are usually paid by the score or ton, their average wages amounting (1849) to about 4s. per day of twelve hours.

OPENCAST.—A cutting in stone, coal, &c., usually in the bottom of a place where a ridge has been passed over, and where it is less expensive to cut down the whole of the ridge to make a uniform roadway or rolleyway than to drive a stone drift through it.

OUTBURST, OUTCROP.—The rising out of a stratum to the surface, or its appearance at the surface in consequence of the denudation of the latter, or in a cliff.

OUTBYE.—Towards the shaft.

OUTBYE-SIDE.—Nearer to the shaft than any other place with which it is compared.

OUTSET.—"An artificial elevation of the ground or an erection of timber or stone round the mouth of a sinking pit to facilitate the disposal of the debris produced in sinking." (*Nicholson.*) To outset water is to put in a column of tubbing, behind which a feeder of water will rise to its level, and require no further dealing with.

OUTSTROKE.—(See *Instroke, Rent.*)

OVERCAST, OVERGATE.—(See *Crossing.*)

OVERLAP.—A reversed hitch. When the hade of a slip makes an acute angle with the floor of the place that has reached it, the hitch is almost invariably a down-throw. In some districts, as in Somersetshire, there are a great number of instances where the contrary is largely the case. In Northumberland and Durham this exception has been found, but it is very rare. In such cases the seam is "overlapped" or doubled.

OVERMAN.—The person who, beneath the viewer, has the charge of the workings of a colliery where there is no under-viewer. He sets the pit to work each morning, and attends to all the detail of arranging the work, and getting the coals each man works to the shaft bottom. It is also his duty to see that each working place is properly ventilated and in a safe state. He also keeps a daily account of the work wrought, and of the whole of the underground expenses and wages, and gives into the colliery office a fortnightly account of the same, the bill containing the amount earned by each man, or set of men if in partnership, and boy during that time. There is one overman to a pit, so that if there are two or three pits at a colliery, there are two or three overmen. An overman is almost invariably a man who has passed through all the gradations of pit work, from the trapper upwards, and who has been raised to his situation on account of his ability and steadiness. His wages in 1849 were £6s. to 28s. per week, with house, garden, and coals gratis.

OVERWORKINGS.—(See *Rent.*)

PACK-WALLS.—(See *Long Work.*) Also band or rubbish built or stowed up behind a face of long work.

PAIR OF GEARS.—(See *Gallows Timber.*)

PANNEL WORK.—The division of a colliery into districts (or pannels) separated from each other by barriers of coal, except where communications are indispensable, with the intention of confining the results of an explosion to the district in which it takes place.

PARROT COAL.—Nearly the same with cannel coal, which see.

PARTING.—A separation between any two beds or layers of coal in the same seam, but without any band.

PEAS.—A description of small coals, smaller than beans, and also produced from the duff.

PEE-DEE.—" A lad employed on board of a keel." (*Nicholson.*)

PICK.—An implement used in hewing coal. It consists of an iron head, 18 inches long, and sharp at each end, and weighing from 3 to 6 lbs. In the centre of the head is wedged a shaft or handle of ash, of the length of $2\frac{1}{2}$ feet. The hewer finds his own picks, but has them sharpened and set out for him by the colliery smith (called the "pick sharper") employed for the purpose, paying to him in return 1d. per fortnight.

PICTURE.—" A covering of sheet iron or brattice deals hung from the roof and shaft-framing to protect the onsetters from the dripping of water at the shaft bottom." (*Nicholson.*) A similar cover to protect the hewer from water which falls from the roof in wet working.

PILLAR.—An oblong or square mass of coal contained between two boards and two headways courses, and left during the first working for the support of the roof. Pillars vary from 20 to 40 yards in length, and from 2 to 20 yards in thickness. When left so thin as 2 or 3 yards, they are not, unless the mine is very shallow indeed, intended to be worked away.

PILLARING.—The building up of stone fallen from the roof by the side of any way required to be left open.

PILLAR WORKING.—(See *Broken.*)

PIT.—A circular, oval, square, or oblong, vertical sinking from the surface. The term shaft, which is often used as synonymous, may either be a pit, or only a portion of one, severed off by means of a vertical or main brattice. Thus: "a pit divided by a brattice into two shafts, *viz.*, a coal and an engine or water shaft," is a correct expression.

PIT HEAP.—(See *Heapstead.*)

PIT HOOK.—(See *Clippers.*)

PLACING WORK.—The direction given by the overman as to the arrangements for the day; also an operation performed by the craneman for the purpose of ascertaining the proportion of the tubs or corves hewed, and from whence each barrowman shall put. The putters at the flat cavil at the commencement of each week (or longer period as the custom of the colliery may be) for the "going"; the first cavil being "first placed"; the second "second placed," etc.; the first placed putting from the hewer nearest and furthest from the flat; the second, from the nearest but one, and furthest but one, etc.; and the last placed, in consequence, getting all his work from the "middle sheth," as the mid number between the nearest and the furthest places is called. The arrangement is made as follows: the cranemen places the men's names in their order, commencing with the nearest, vertically upon the chalking deal, with the number of tubs each man is allowed to hew, so that each may have a fair share of the work to be done; the tubs are then added up, and divided by the number of putters, which gives the quantity each putter is to put, if hewed; half of this quantity is then taken by the craneman, and is made up from the nearest hewers, and the other half from the furthest, and this is the "first placed's (he is called, " first placeder ") work. If any coals are left of the work of the nearest and furthest hewers, they form the commencement of the quantity to be put by the "second placed " (" second placeder "), and so on.

PLATE.—Metal—Blue or Grey shale :—the term "plate" was first used about 35 or 40 years ago, to describe bricks ("plate bricks") made from metal or shale. "*Plate*," in the Western parts of the Counties, particularly in the lead mining districts, means the same as regards strata, as *Metal* in the colliery districts.

PLATE NAILS.—Used in laying tram plates or bridge rails, to nail the plates or rails to the sleepers. They weigh about 22 to the pound; are from 2 to $2\frac{1}{2}$ inches long, and are made with flat countersunk heads, round shafts, and flat points.

PLUG AND FEATHER.—(See *Fox wedge.*)

PLUNGER.—(See *Forcing set.*)

POST.—Sandstone. (*Hazle* of the lead districts.)

POUT, PUNCH.—A tool used by the deputies in drawing timber out of a dangerous place. It has a shank about 8 feet long with a spade handle, and a head, pointed and slightly curved towards the handle at one side, and like a hammer at the other; it is either used as a ram to knock the props down, or to draw them out after they have been knocked down; it is supported by a hook and chain when in use.

POWDER.—Gunpowder: used coarse for blasting, fine for charging kitties.

PRICKER.—A rod of copper, about a quarter of an inch in diameter at the thick end, at which it is turned round into a ring, and tapering to a point at the other; it is about 3 feet long. The point is inserted into the cartridge for blasting, and by it the cartridge is put into its place in the drill hole; the pricker being allowed to remain in the hole until it is stemmed or tamped up with small shale or metal. The stemming should be damped. After being stemmed the pricker is steadily drawn out by the ring, thus leaving a port-hole to the gunpowder, by means of which, with a kitty and match, the powder is ignited (1849). Frequent accidents having occurred by the ignition of the gunpowder from sparks occasioned by the attrition of an iron pricker against stone or pyrites, the use of iron for the purpose is forbidden by law (Mines Act, 1872.) Copper is not absolutely safe.

PRICKING.—A thin layer of soft coaly shale often found between the bottom of a seam of coal and the regular floor. It is used to "prick" in—in kirving—and is advantageous to the hewer.

PROP.—A piece of unsawn wood, cut 2½ or 3 inches shorter than the thickness of the seam of coal, and set upright beneath the end of a crowntree, or under a headtree for the support of the roof. Props are best made of peeled larch when this can be obtained. Where the wood is not less than 3 inches in diameter, they are worth, when of Scotch and larch fir mixed, about 4/- per 72 feet (1849.) The supply which used to be principally from Scotland having fallen short, it is now mainly obtained from Norway and Sweden; and the use of cast and wrought iron, particularly for permanent propping, as in rolley ways, is advancing.

PROP MAUL.—An iron maul, with an ash handle 3 feet long, used by the deputies in drawing or setting props.

PROVE.—To ascertain the position of a seam of coal when it has been thrown downwards or upwards by a slip, or the nature of the strata in a district, by boring or sinking.

PULLEYS.—The wheels placed above a pit, over which the ropes for drawing coals, etc., are passed. They should seldom be less than 10 feet diameter; they are, sometimes, more than 20. They should, as a rule, be of the same diameter as the average diameter of the rope roll. They should be placed as low as is consistent with safety, on account of the angle of the ropes.

PULLEY FRAMES.—The gearing above a pit upon which the pulleys are supported; they were formerly constructed altogether of timber, they are now frequently of iron.

PUMPS.—(See *Forcing set; Lifting set.*)

PUNCH-PROP.—A short prop, set upon a crowntree or balk, where it does not support the middle of the roof on account of the roof having fallen before the timber was set. Also a short prop, about 14 or 15 inches long, placed by a hewer under his sump or back-end when there is any danger of its dropping down before he has got it kirved sufficiently far. It is best always to set these, whether danger is apprehended or not. (See *Back—Sprags.*)

PUTTER.—(See *Barrowman.*)

PUTTING PONIES.—Ponies 10 or 11 hands high used in substitution for putters or barrowmen.

QUADRANT.—A beam constructed with one half at right angles with the other half, like the letter ∟. It is used for converting a horizontal into a vertical motion, as in the case of an engine being required to pump from a shaft at some distance from it. It is frequently made double acting as in ⊥, spears being hung on each end. The horizontal spear from the engine is attached to the top of the vertical leg.

QUARL.—A flag made of burnt fire-clay, used for flooring coke ovens, and other purposes.

RAG-PUMP, RAG-WHEEL PUMP.—A pump used in early coal mining for lifting water by manual labour from small depths. It consisted of a pipe with an endless chain with discs of iron and leather attached to it at short distances apart, which when moving upwards lifted the water by means of the discs, which passing over a wheel above the top of the pump, returned down to the water outside of the pipe. Bastier's patent chain pump is an adaptation of the chain wheel principle.

RAKE.—A rake with about 8 teeth, 2 inches apart, and 3 inches long, used by the hewer in working coal by separation; the shaft may be 3 feet long.

RAM.—(See *Forcing Set.*)

RAMBLE. — Called also FOLLOWING STONE. — A thin stratum of shale or post, often found lying immediately above a seam of coal. It falls down, and getting mixed with the coals, causes some trouble to the hewer, in getting it separated and cast back. At some collieries, an extra allowance of 3d. or 4d. per score is made for hewing with ramble; at others, the nature of the coal with all its inconveniences, is taken into account in the hewing price.

RAPPER.—A lever placed at the top and bottom of a shaft or inclined plane, or engine plane, connected with a wire placed between the two. Its use is to signal by means of a hammer or bell.

RECKONING DAY.—" The day on which the workmen receive their pay-notes or checks from the overman showing the amount each man or each set of men is entitled to receive for the fortnight, usually two days before the pay day." (*Nicholson.*)

REFUGE STALLS.—Man-holes required by law to be made in engine or self-acting planes and horse roads for retreat during the passing of the trains.

REGULATOR.—A frame containing a sort of door, one half of which slides open past the other half, like a transom window. It is placed in that division of air which has least distance to travel; the use of the slide being to regulate the quantity of air travelling in that direction. A row of holes should be made in the middle batten of the sliding part, and one in the middle stanchion of the frame, so that the regulator may be locked by means of a screw bolt in the proper position, to prevent it from being ignorantly or wilfully altered. An ordinary door with a sliding shutter in it to allow a portion of air to pass, is called a *regulating door.*

RENK OR RANK.—A standard distance of 60 or 80 yards (called the first renk), upon which a standard price is paid for putting a score of coals. This, for 20 peck tubs and 80 yards varies from 1s. to 1s. 3d. per score, the height and inclination of the seam being taken into account; and an increased payment of 1d. per score is made for every addition of 20 yards to the first renk. The renk is measured by the overman in the middle of the fortnight; the average distance from the flat or station to each working place being taken, commencing to measure from the middle of the station, and the score price for putting for that fortnight calculated thereon.

RENT.—Colliery rent consists of a fixed or certain rent, in consideration of which a certain quantity of coals is allowed to be annually worked, or worked and vended, but paid whether that quantity is worked, or worked and vended, or not; and also of a surplus or tentale rent, payable for the coal worked, or worked and vended—above the certain quantity. It is usually covenanted that if the quantity worked, or worked and vended, in any year, shall fall short of that allowed in consideration of the certain rent, such "short workings," as they are called, shall be allowed rent-free in future years, when the quantity worked shall exceed that allowed for the certain rent. Excess above the certain quantity is called "over-workings." When the rent is chargeable upon the coal *worked*, there is allowed free, a suitable per centage for engines, workmen, &c. When it is chargeable upon the *coals worked and sold*, no charge is made for consumption at the colliery. There are also :—

Outstroke Rent, for the privilege of breaking the barrier, and working and conveying underground the coal from an adjoining royalty.

Shaft Rent, for the privilege of drawing up the shaft the coal worked from another royalty by outstroke.

Wayleave Rent, for the privilege of conveying, over the surface, from the pit to the boundary, coal worked from another royalty by out-stroke, and drawn up the pit. Wayleave may be charged by any proprietor across whose land he may allow coal, &c., to pass.

Damaged Ground Rent, usually double agricultural rent for land occupied by engines, heapstead, shops, houses, railways, &c.

RETURN.—The airway by which the air returns to the upcast shaft after it has left the working places.

RIDE.—To go to bank.

RIDER.—Sometimes, at a hitch, there is only a slipping of one fractured edge of the coal past the other, but sometimes these are separated by mineral matter of various composition, often soft clayey shale, called the rider; also called the gowk of the trouble.

RING.—A crib laid in a pit to collect water. (See *Crib*.)

RISE.—To the rise of; above the level of.

RISER.—A hitch which throws up the coal in the same direction as the drift which approached it.

ROBBING.—(See *Broken*.)

ROLL.—(See *Balk*.)

ROLLERS.—Made usually of metal, sometimes of hard wood, and placed upon inclined or other planes, to support the ropes and remove the friction which would be occasioned by their dragging along the way.

ROLLEY.—A carriage used formerly to carry tubs or corves along the horse-roads underground. The rolley was contrived as an improvement upon the tram upon which a single corf was placed; a horse drawing one, two, or three corves at a time. Upon the rolley, which travelled upon larger wheels, and on round topped rails instead of tram plates, two, or in some cases, three corves were placed, the horse drawing two or three rolleys. A further improvement took place, when the rolley-ways were constructed more perfectly; and in some rare cases, as many as 7 rolleys with 21 tubs of coals, each full tub weighing 12 cwt. have been the draught of a good pit-horse. Rolleys have given way to tubs on their own wheels, from 20 to 25 of which upon a carefully laid and well kept way, and containing 8 cwt. each, can be drawn by a good horse.

The following is given as the regular daily work of 12 hours of a good pit horse, upon a level rolley-way, in a good state—

EMPTY LOAD.

	lbs.	
9 rolleys, weighing 7½ cwt. each, 27 journeys of 500 yards, equal to	204,120,	led 500 yards.
18 empty tubs, weighing 2½ cwt. each, 27 journeys of 500 yards, equal to	136,080	,,

FULL LOAD.

9 rolleys, as above	204,120	,,
18 full tubs, weighing 9½ cwt. each, distance as above	517,104	,,

Total weight equal...1,061,424, led 500 yards.

And taking the fraction at 1·130th part, or one half of that of common tub-way (see *Barrowman*), the power of the horse is found to be for 8 hours equal to 25,515 lbs. raised one foot high per minute.

According to Desaguliers, a horse drawing a weight out of a well over a pulley can raise 200 lbs. for 8 hours together, at the rate of 2½ miles per hour, equal to 44,000 lbs. raised one foot high per minute. Mr. Smeaton states the efficiency of a horse at 22,000 lbs. raised one foot high per minute. The ordinary estimate of engineers is 33,000 lbs.

ROLLEY-WAY.—The horse road underground.

ROLLEY-WAY MAN.—A man whose business it is to attend to the rolley-way and keep it in order. It is also his duty to keep away the work, and see that no time is lost in getting the full waggons to the shaft and the empty ones in-bye again. His wages are about 2s. 9d. for 8 hours, or 3s. 4d. if he stands 12 hours (1849.)

ROOF STONE.—The stratum lying immediately above the coal.

ROPE.—Pit ropes were formerly all made of hemp, and previous to about 60 years ago, were generally round. They are now almost entirely made of steel or iron wire. The first wire ropes used for winding, following the then form of hemp ropes were made flat, four or six ropes, laid side by side, being stitched together with iron wires; but where the position of the winding engine, with regard to the pit will allow, round ropes are now almost always adopted. In several cases, however, where the winding engine has been placed very near the pit, so as to be employed in pumping, flat ropes are used. Hauling ropes, both above and under ground, are now also of steel or iron. Crab ropes are generally of hemp, but those of steel or iron wire are rapidly taking their place. Each round wire rope is usually manufactured with 6 strands, each strand containing 6 wires, with a hempen or wire core.

In the year 1842, the price paid at a Durham colliery for a round wire rope weighing 6 lbs. to the fathom, and having 7 wires in each strand, was 77s. 6d. per cwt.; and for a round wire rope weighing $6\frac{1}{4}$ lbs. to the fathom, and having 6 wires in each strand, it was 75s. 0d. per cwt.

ROPE ROLL.—A cylinder fixed upon the main shaft of the winding engine, upon which the ropes used in drawing coals are wound. In the case of *Flat rope rolls* there are two compartments, or planes, each of a little more width than the breadth of the rope, upon which the rope coils and uncoils, being kept in its place by side arms or horns. The diameter of a flat rope roll should not be less than 8 feet, and may, with advantage, be 10 or even 15 feet or more.

A *Scroll drum* is constructed of a comparatively small diameter at the sides, the diameter increasing rapidly towards the centre part which is level, the rope travelling on scrolls of iron mounting up from taking the lift at the bottom towards the top, and continuing to coil for a few turns upon the level portion of the drum, the object being to counterbalance the ropes.

In a *Conical drum* the diameter of the drum in the

middle is greater than that at the sides, the drum surface being plain.

In a *Parallel drum* the diameter is the same all across. With this form of rope roll, a rope similar in weight to the winding rope, one end of which is attached to the bottom of the cage at bank, and the other end to the bottom of the cage at the bottom, and allowed to hang freely in the sump forms a complete balance weight. This form has always been adopted in the water balance pits of South Wales—chains, however, being altogether used both above and below the cages : it would probably be better to substitute chain for rope in the above case.

ROUND COALS.—Best coals, from which the small has been separated by skreening.

ROUNDER.—(See *Bore.*)

ROW AND STOWCHES.—(Roll and Stanchions ?) (See *Jack Roll.*)

ROYALTY.—The minerals with the right of working them. They presumably belong to the owner of the freehold, except in the case of royal mines, from the surface to the centre of the earth. The ownership of the surface may be vested in one person, and of the mines in another. In the case of copyhold and customary lands, the right of *property* in minerals is vested in the lord of the manor, and the right of *possession* is vested in the tenant of the surface, and consequently, in such cases, neither the lord nor the tenant can exercise any right to work them without mutual consent. (*Bainbridge's Law of Mines and Minerals.*)

RUNNER.—(See *Bore.*)

RUNNING BALK.—A balk set in the direction of a drift, at its side instead of across it, to form a support for the cross balks. A running balk at each side, with balks or planks supported by them is the common method of timbering through an old board or place where the roof has fallen so heavily as to make the entire ridding of the fall too expensive.

RUNNING FITTER.—The subordinate of a fitter; he looks out for orders from shippers.

SAFETY LAMP.—(See *Davy*.)

SAGRE, or SEGGAR, CLAY.—Fire-clay; argillaceous and siliceous shale used for making fire-bricks; it is usually the thill of a seam of coal; it abounds in stigmaria rootlets.

SAND.—"The sand" which is seen in Northumberland and Durham, is a stratum of soft sandstone underlying the magnesian limestone. When it contains much water, it wastes or falls away to a soft loose quicksand, and where, as in some instances the quantity of water to be contended with is very large, it sometimes presents difficulties in sinking through it which are almost insurmountable.

SCABBY.—(See *Claggy*.)

SCAFFOLD.—A wooden platform fixed accross a shaft. In the case of a permanently abandoned pit, where it is not filled up from the bottom, a scaffold is sometimes put in, a few fathoms from the top, above which the pit is filled up. As the wood decays in time, the scaffold falls in with its covering. Such scaffolds, if put in at all, should be secure domes, built with masonry on good foundations.

SCALE.—A scale of air is a portion allowed to escape through a door, or stopping, for the purpose of ventilating a waggon or rolley-way, &c.

SCALLOP, SKELP.—To use the pick in pulling down or hewing coal instead of kirving, nicking, and wedging, or bringing it down with powder, &c.

SCAMY POST.—Soft short jointy freestone, in very thin layers, and much mixed with mica.

SCARES.—Thin layers of pyrites or spar, interstratified in coal seams, or similar layers of coal found in post or metal.

SCORE.—A standard number of tubs or corves of coal at each colliery, upon which the hewers' and putters' prices for working are paid, called the score price. It varies in different localities from 20 to 26 tubs. Thus on the Tyne, the score consists of 20 ; on the Wear, 21 ; and on the Tees, from 20 to 26 tubs, at different collieries.

SCORE PRICE.—(See *Score*.)

SCOTCH.—A piece of wood of triangular section with a handle to it placed on the rail before the front wheel of a waggon, or set for the purpose of a gradual arrest of motion.

SCRAPER.—"A round iron rod about $\frac{1}{4}$ in. in diameter, and 3 feet long, turned up flat at each end and used for cleaning the coal dust out of a drill hole." (*Nicholson*.) The scraper is used also for pushing loose powder into the hole when it is used in this state. The same precaution which is required in the case of the pricker, is ordered by the Mines Act, 1888, by the prohibition of steel or iron for this purpose.

SCUTTLE OR SCOOP.—Used for filling water from the face of a dip place, or sump into a water tub ; it is usually made with wooden sides and back, and a thin sheet iron bottom. The sides, to the bottom of which, as well as to the bottom of the back the sheet iron is nailed, are at the back end of the same depth as the back, and at the front end gradually curve up to the level of the top of the back. The top is also partly covered from the top of the back forwards, with wood, and in the middle of the back is an iron handle ; it may be made 20 inches long, 12 inches broad, and 6 inches deep at the back.

SEAM.—A bed of coal.

SEG.—To bend down, as a plank or balk does at its middle by superincumbent weight.

SELF-ACTING INCLINE.—(See *Incline*.)

SEPARATION.—Filling round coals only, the small being separated and cast back in the mine.

SET.—To fill a tub unfairly, the large coals being built up and left intentionally hollow in the tub or corf, and carefully filled over the top, the object being to get full payment for as small as possible a quantity of coals. This fraud can only be practised where the hewers are paid by measure; in place of which payment by weight is now, with a slight exception, the only legal mode. Also a train of tubs or waggons. Also a column of pumps.

SET OUT.—A tub or corf of coals filled insufficiently, and consequently forfeited.

SETTERS.—Large pieces of coal; so called by the landsale cartmen, from their use in piling or setting round the sides of their carts, to enable them to hold a larger quantity of coals than could otherwise be placed upon them; the smaller coals being put in the centre.

SETTLE BOARDS or SADDLE BOARDS.—The portion of the heapstead at the top of the shaft, and between it and the skreens, covered with iron or metal sheets (see *Flat Sheets.*)

SHACKLE.—A turned bar of iron, the long, flattened and shaped ends of which are rivetted, or collared on, to the turned back and swelled end of a rope, forming at the end an eye by which it is attached to the cage chains, etc.; or to another rope, in which case there are two shackles; these ropes are said to be socketted. Also a horse shoe link, with a bolt through eyes at its open end.

SHAFT.—(See *Pit.*)—Also the handle of a pick, hack shovel, or maul.

SHAFT FRAME.—(See *Heapstead.*)

SHAFT PILLARS or SHAFT WALLS.—(See *Holing About.*)

SHAFT RENT.—(See *Rent.*)

SHAM DOOR.—(See *Regulator.*)

SHEAR LEGS.—(See *Bore.*)—Also two long legs of timber or iron (set over an engine-pit), over which is placed a crosshead or crowntree upon which, and at the bottom of one of the legs, is placed a strong sheave. The crab rope passes under the latter and over the former of these sheaves, and is used by means of the crab for lowering or raising spears or pumps, changing buckets, etc.

SHEATHING, SHEETING.—(See *Tubbing.*)

SHEAVE.—The wheel round which the rope of a self-acting inclined plane, or the tail rope of an engine plane runs; the speed at which the set upon the incline runs being regulated by a lever attached to a brake which acts upon a crib placed upon the sheave for the purpose; also a grooved wheel used in place of a roller to guide or alter the direction of a rope.

SHELL: BUCKET SHELL or CLACK SHELL.—A bucket or clack before it is grathed.

SHETH DOOR.—(See *Door.*)

SHETH STOPPING.—(See *Coursing.*)

SHETHING.—(See *Coursing.*)

SHETHS.—The ribs of a chaldron or other waggon.

SHIFT.—The time worked by a man, or set of men, at coal or other underground work. A shift is 8 hours long, except in sinking, where it is 4 hours. The payment for off-hand work, such as waste work, timbering, ridding, etc., is 3s. 0d. per shift of 8 hours; for the sinker's shift of 4 hours it is 2s. 0d. (1849.) The sinker, however, generally returns at the end of 8 hours to another 4 hours' shift. When a colliery is worked by two sets of hewers, each working for 8 hours, one set following the other, the first set is called the fore-shift and the second the back-shift.

SHIFTERS.—Men paid by the day for doing shift work.

SHIFT-WORK.—Work paid for by the day or shift.

SHINGLY COALS.—(See *Chinley Coal.*)

SHIVERY POST.—(See *Scamy.*)

SHOOTING-FAST.—Blowing down coal with gunpowder, without nicking, by which the coals are produced in a very inferior condition.

SHORT WORKINGS or SHORTS.—(See *Rent.*)

SHOT.—The cartridge, or portion of gunpowder used in blasting. It is put into a cartridge made of brown paper by folding it round a shot stick. The cartridge is about 1 inch in diameter, and from 4 to 9 or 10 inches long, or longer if required. A pound of gunpowder will make 5 six inch shots.

SHOT STICK.—(See *Shot.*)

SHOW.—The pale blue "top," or lambent flame, which appears above the ordinary flame of a candle, when it is burning in an atmosphere mixed with fire-damp. A mixture of carbonic acid with the fire-damp, occasions the colour of the "top" to be brown, and much longer and more distinct. When both the fire-damp and the air with which it is mixed are pure, the "top" is very faint; and great caution and care are required in making the examination. It is by the show upon the candle that the presence of fire-damp may be detected, but it is now the practice to make such examinations with a safety lamp.

SIDDLE.—The inclination of a seam of coal.

SIDE OVER.—To drive headways course across a pillar of coal in working the broken.

SIDE-WAVERS.—The loose sides of a drift or open-cast, which would if unsupported soon fall. It is best to remove them altogether. They generally occur when a crush is taking place.

SIDING.—A bye-way or passing place.

SINK.—To make a pit. (See *Pit.*)

SINKER.—(See *Shift.*)

SINKING SET.—(See *Crab.*)

SIPING.—A small issue of water without pressure.

SKELPING.—(See *Scallop.*)

SKIPPER.—The captain or master of a keel.

SKREEN.—A frame 4 or 5 feet wide, and 11 to 15 feet long, the upper side of which inclines from the hempstead to the top of the coal waggon; it is furnished with iron or metal bars placed at the distance of from $\frac{3}{8}$ to $\frac{3}{4}$ of an inch apart, upon which the coals are teemed as they are drawn out of the pit. The coals which pass over the skreen are sent away as best skreened coals; and the small coal which passes through the bars falls into the duff box, from whence it is taken to the apparatus.

SKREEN MEN or SKREENERS.—Men who pass the coals over the skreens into the wagons, and clean them from stones, slates, brasses, &c. They should be paid in proportion to the quantity of dirt picked out from among the coals. Their wages are about 2s. 6d. to 2s. 8d. per day of 12 hours (1849.)

SLAG.—(See *Brat.*)

SLED or SLEDGE.—(See *Barrowman.*)

SLEEPER.—Tram and rolley-way sleepers are pieces of wood about $2\frac{1}{2}$ to $3\frac{1}{2}$ feet long, about 6 inches broad, and 2 or $2\frac{1}{2}$ inches thick, for nailing tram plates or bridge nails to, or chairs for edge or round-topped rolley-way rails. They are best made of larch.

SLIDES.—Upright rails, of wood or metal, fixed in a shaft for the purpose of guiding the cages, which have corresponding shoes or grooves attached to them. They are now frequently made of wire rope, passing through eyes attached to the cages. They are also made with round topped iron or steel railway rails partly clasped by jaws upon the cages: with these, two guides on one side of each cage are quite sufficient.

SLIDING DEALS or STRIKING DEALS. — Deals placed diagonally from the balk placed across the top of a sinking pit (upon the planking resting upon which and the edge of the shaft the sinking kibbles or tubs are landed), to or towards the wall side of the pit under the planking to guide the tubs on to the pit top.

SLIDING SCALE.—" A scale agreed to between masters and men by which wages are regulated according to the selling price of coals, or according to the amount realized on the sale of the coals ; also a scale whereby the hewer's tonnage or score price is regulated by the height of the seam " (*Nicholson*); or by the thickness of band.

SLINGS.—"Chains used for convenience in raising or lowering heavy weights." (*Nicholson.*)

SLIP.—(See *Hitch.*)

SLIVER.—A thin lath, placed within two groves, cut lengthways for the purpose, in the edges of two planks, intended to be joined together for the purpose of making the joint air or water-tight.

SLUDGER.—(See *Bore.*)

SMALL COALS.—Coals that pass through the skreen bars before further separation.

SMALL LEADER.—A lad employed to put small coals to a stowboard.

SMART MONEY.—5s. per week paid to men, and 2s. 6d. per week paid to lads, disabled by accident whilst at work in the pit.

SNAP.—"A small flat pointed pick used on the skreens for chipping off brasses, stone, or band from large coals." (*Nicholson.*)

SNORE-HOLES.—At the bottom of a set of pumps is a short piece called a wind-bore cast with round holes, through which the water passes, and through the clack to the bucket when raised in pumping. In a sinking pit these holes are plugged above the level, beyond which it is required that the water should not rise. When the level of the water is lowered to the top of the holes, the air "snores" at the top of the holes—whence the name.

SNOT.—The cauliflower top of a candle wick.

SOAMS.—(See *Headsman.*)

SOCKET.—(See *Shackle.*)

SOLE.—The part of a waggon or tub frame to which the bearings of the wheels are attached, and into which the sheths are inserted.

SOOTY COAL.—Dull, danty, soft coal often found near a hitch.

SPARE.—A piece of wood, 6 or 8 inches long, and 6 inches broad, cut from 1 inch Scotch deal, with one of the sides tapered off to the end; used for driving behind cribs or tubbing. A baff end being put in first behind the crib or tubbing, and next to the pit wall, and the spare driven between, in the manner of a wedge.

SPEAR PLATES.—(See *Spears*.)

SPEARS.—The rod of a pump. Spears are made of Memel, or Norway fir, or pitch pine, in lengths of about 40 feet, and joined together with spear plates, which are flat plates of forged iron, say 14 feet long, $4\frac{1}{2}$ to $5\frac{1}{2}$ in. broad, 1 to $1\frac{1}{4}$ in. thick in middle, and $\frac{1}{2}$ to $\frac{5}{8}$ in. thick at ends, and 10 bolts in each pair of plates, with cross bolts called clinch or clink bolts to keep the whole firmly bound and prevent stripping. Wet spears are those which, working within a column of pumps are constantly immersed in water; dry spears are those which pass down to the top of each set; in a forcing set, the whole of the spears are dry spears.

SPIGOT AND FAUCIT.—A description of pump joint in which each pump (or pipe) is cast with a cup or faucit end. The other or spigot end, being plain, for the purpose of insertion into the cup, the joint being made tight by wedging between the inside of the cup and the spigot. It makes an excellent joint, but requires more putting together than a flanch joint, and is also much more difficult to break should it be necessary to do so.

SPILE WEDGES.—Half wedges. A course of these is driven into the packing behind a wedging crib after it has received as many full-sized wedges as can be driven in. (See *Wedge*.)

SPLINT.—Coarse grey-looking coal. It burns to white ashes; it is suitable for burning lime, and the better sorts are well adapted to steam purposes.

SPLIT.—To divide the current of air which has descended the down cast shaft into principal and subordinate currents for the purpose of supplying the various districts with distinct currents of fresh air.

SPOUT.—(See *Staiths.*)

SPRAG.—(See *Drag.*)

SPRAGS.—Short props placed under the coal at the front of a kirving as a precaution against its premature fall.

SPRING BEAMS.—Strong balks of timber placed on each side of the beam of a pumping engine at such a level as that if a breakage of the spears were to take place, the inner stroke of the engine would be arrested before the piston descended upon the cylinder bottom. The spring beams also extend beyond the engine-house to the outer end of the beam. The catch-pin (see *Catch-pin*) does not fall direct upon these balks, but upon others placed above them, which being sloped up at the underside towards the ends, form a spring which softens the fall.

SPRING HOOK.—(See *Clippers.*)

STAITHS.—"1709. From the state of the trade it was necessary to hold, from time to time, large stocks of coals, in order to give dispatch, to suit tides, and to meet other emergencies. Hence those extensive erections called Staiths, many of which remain to the present day." (*Dunn, View of the Coal Trade,* 1844.)

Very few of these now exist.

The term staith is now applied to the whole of the erections constructed for the shipment of coals, whether they be capable of being used as coal depôts or not. The general principle upon which they are now constructed, consists in having a frame upon which the full waggon of coals rests, which is carried down or dropped to the deck of the vessel by the weight of the waggon, its motion being retarded by a balance weight, which is sufficient, after the coals have been discharged from the waggon by the off putter, to raise it up again to the level of the railway from which it descended. In some cases the waggon is not lowered down to the deck as above, but the coals are dropped through the bottom board into an open topped, but otherwise closed spout, with a slide at the bottom;

in the former case the staith is called a *drop*, and in the latter, a *spout*. The spout is often close-topped.

STAMP.—A hole made with the pick point in the coal in which the wedge is fixed before driving with the maul.

STANDAGE.—A portion of workings excavated on the dip side of an engine pit, as a reservoir for the mine water, during a suspension of the pumping engine from work. A drift, called an underlevel drift is driven perfectly level in the stone beneath the seam, between the lowest point of the standage and a point above the bottom of the sump; and a dam is placed in it containing a plug hole or screw valve, which is closed when the engine is stopped, and opened when pumping is resumed. A good standage is of the utmost importance to the well-being of a colliery.

STANDARD WEIGHT.—(See *Average*.)

STANDING BOBBY.—A fast shot. A shot which blows out the stemming only. It may arise from the shot being too light; or from having been insufficiently stemmed; or from the hole having been drilled too far; called also a blown out shot.

STANDING FIRE.—Where the solid coal has become ignited, and the only means of extinguishing it is by barring it off with air tight stoppings or dams, until the carbonic acid produced has destroyed all combustion; it is necessary to put a pipe into such dams, the pipe end being bent down under water to allow of the escape of gas, but not of the re-entry of air. In South Staffordshire where "gob fire" is very common, it has been found by practice that the most effectual dam is made with sand.

STANDING SET.—In sinking with pumps when the sinking set has become of sufficient length, the top standing set is placed in a cistern which stands on a strong oak bunton or iron girder set across the pit, and pumps to bank the water delivered into it by the sinking set continued downwards with the sinking.

STANDING SET BUNTON.—(See *Standing Set*.)

STANDING SET CISTERN.—(See *Standing Set.*)

STAPLE.—A small pit, sunk upwards or downwards, from one seam to another, or for the purpose of proving a slip dyke. A counterbalance staple is a small pit sunk from the surface for a balance weight to work in, in order to assist the winding engine by equalizing the weight of the ascending and descending ropes. The arrangement is as follows :—The rope to which the balance weight is attached is of such a length, that as the ascending and descending cages approach each other the balance weight, which consists of a very heavy chain, shall gradually, by resting on the bottom of the staple, relieve the winding engine of its weight, so that at meetings, when the ropes themselves balance each other, no influence shall be exerted by the balance weight. After meetings, the descending rope becomes heaviest, and the engine again winds up the balance weight to counteract its downward impulse, in the same manner as, by formerly unwinding it, the ascending rope was assisted. In the case of flat ropes, the winding engines in a great measure possess a balancing power within themselves, by the ascending rope gradually increasing its coil, and the descending one diminishing it. A rope or chain equal in weight to the winding rope per fathom, and of suitable length, one end of which is attached to the bottom of one cage and one to the bottom of the other, with a parallel drum is a perfect balance weight. (See *Rope Roll*). A jack-head staple is sunk for the jack-head or high set of pumps to work in, when the pumping engine has a back beam.

START.—(See *Gin.*)

STATION.—(See *Crane.*)

STEAM JET.—A mode of ventilation invented by Mr. Goldsworthy Gurney, and first applied to the ventilation of collieries by the late Mr. T. E. Forster, in 1848, by which an air current was produced by the escape of high pressure steam through small orifices; the mode of action being similar to that of the blast pipe in a locomotive engine.

STEEL MILL.—A contrivance used, before the invention of the safety lamp, to give light in foul places. " It is an instrument for striking light with flint and steel. A brass wheel about 5 inches diameter, with 52 teeth, works a pinion with 11 teeth; on the axle of the latter is fixed a thin steel wheel from 5 to 6 inches in diameter. The wheels are placed in a light frame of iron, which is suspended by a leather belt round the neck of the person who *plays* the mill. Great velocity is given to the steel wheel by turning the handle of the toothed wheel; and the sharp edge of a flint is applied to the circumference of the steel wheel, which immediately elicits an abundance of sparks, and emits a considerable light." (*Buddle, First Report.*) The steel mill was said to be the invention of Spedding. The greatest confidence in its safety at one time existed; but it was proved to have been misplaced, for to it several explosions of gas were eventually traced.

STEM.—To tamp or fill up a drill hole in which the powder has been placed previous to blasting.

STEMMER.—(See *Beater.*)

STEMMING.—Small coals or stones with which a drill hole is tamped (1849). By the Coal Mines Regulation Act, 1887, the use for this purpose of coal or coal dust is prohibited. The use of siliceous stemming is dangerous, particularly in post or sandstone, where the hole is charged with loose powder.

STENTING.—An opening between a pair of headways or drifts, through which the air circulates until another is holed further in-bye. Stentings should be holed no more frequently than is rendered necessary by the quantity of gas issued in driving the drifts; because, as they require, on the holing of every new one that the last shall be permanently stopped by a stopping of brick or stone, the too frequent holing of stentings, by increasing the number of stoppings, not only adds to the expense, but increases the liability to loss of air, which at the best stoppings often escapes.

STICK.—To cease work in order to obtain an increase, or prevent a reduction of wages.

STOB AND FEATHER.—(See *Fox Wedge*.)

STOCK.—Colliery stock comprises the establishment of shafts, buildings, engines, waggons, horses, and materials of every description necessary to carry on a colliery. It is divided into—

1.—*Dead Stock*, which consists of such attachments to the freehold, as shafts, engine houses, and other buildings of brick or stone as (in the absence of agreement to the contrary) are the property of the lessor.

2.—*Fixed Stock*: this includes everything, except the foregoing, required to keep the colliery in a working state, such as engines, waggons, railway, tubs, tramway, ways, skreens, &c., and a proper working quantity of horses, hay, corn, timber, oil, nails, &c., &c.

3.—*Movable Stock* consists of what can be sold off the premises without prejudice to the working of the colliery being fully carried on; it can only comprise, therefore, old pumps, unnecessary engines, and useless materials of every description, and resting coals.

It is generally understood that horses, hay and corn, and all materials in store are comprehended in the term movable (or as it is termed "live") stock; but why, if an engine is substituted for a dozen horses, and the work performed the same, the former should be called *fixed*, and the latter *movable*, it is not easy to say.

STONE DRIFT.—A drift in stone from seam to seam, or through a fault.

STONE HEAD.—The top of the solid strata.

STOOK.—A small block or pillar of coal left to support the headways course in taking off a jud or lift in pillar working. When the lift has been got, the stook ought if practicable to be removed.

STOPPING.—A wall built in any excavation for the purpose of conducting air further into the mine. Stopping are built of brick or stone where required to be permanent, the windward side of the stopping being plastered carefully with lime. The best and cheapest stoppings are built of the stone which falls from the roof, when it is not too soft; these should not be less than 4 feet thick. When of brick they may be 9 inches thick. Stone stoppings are superior to brick stoppings, in affording a better support to the roof. All are better for being stowed at the back side. Stoppings which are not required to be permanent, are put up with common brattice, plastered at the joints if necessary, or with brattice cloth. (See *Brattice.*)

STOW.—To put stones and rubbish from falls requiring removal, or from stone drifts, or from where it is taken up or taken down, &c., into places appointed for the purpose.

STOW-BOARD.—A board driven for the convenience of stowage.

STRAW.—(See *Kitty.*)

STRIKE.—Wood-full. In former agreements between coalowners and workmen, it was stipulated that the specified coal tubs should be filled "strike or wood-full."

Also, strike, a more general cessation from labour than implied by stick.

STRUM.—A cover containing small holes placed upon the end of a water pipe at which water enters, to prevent stone or other rubbish passing into the pipe, whereby the passage of the water might be obstructed.

STYTHE.—Carbonic acid gas, often found in old workings, and given off in most shallow mines.

SULPHUR.—A common expression among old miners for fire-damp.

SUMP.—(See *Back-end.*) Also, in driving a stone drift, or in sinking a pit, that portion kept a yard or more in advance of the drift or pit, to enable the gunpowder or other explosive to act with greater advantage upon the parts left. The origin of the term has been in its application to the advanced part of a sinking pit, where the water accumulates, and where the bottom of the sinking set of pumps is placed.

Also, that portion of a pit, beneath the seam of coal or other bottom landing, where the water of the mine gathers in order to be pumped to the surface. Also, a small reservoir, cut by the side of a dip and wet place into which the water from the face of the place is conveyed by means of levels, or by bowling, and afterwards led or pumped by a hand or horse pump to some point whence it will flow to the shaft.

SURFEIT.—The pressure exercised by pent up gas of any kind easing itself off with some force, frequently rending the roof, sides, or floor of the seam ; this often takes place without any sudden outburst of gas.

SWAG.—(See *Seg.*)

SWEEP-PLATES, SWAPES.—Curved plates for laying barrow-way round a turn.

SWALLEY OR SWELLEY.—A gradual depression or dish in the strata. In the bottom of the dish the seam of coal is usually thicker.

SWING DOOR.—(See *Door.*)

SWITCH.—A movable pointed rail, by the turning of which a set of tubs is diverted from the main to a branch way.

TACK.—A small prop of coal sometimes left in kirving a jud to support it until the kirving is finished, except knocking out the tack. A punch prop is commonly used for the same purpose.

TAIL CRAB.—(See *Crab, Fleet.*)

TAIL ROPE.—(See *Engine Plane.*)

TARE.—(See *Average Weight.*)

TEEM BYE.—To teem the coals over the resting coal stock or heap when there are no waggons.

TEN.—A measure of coals upon which the lessor's rent is paid. It usually consists of 440 bolls of 8 pecks each, but varies under different landlords, generally within the range of from 418 to 440 bolls; it rises, however, as high as 550 bolls. As the weight of a boll of coals (See *Chaldron*) is 2·35284 cwts., the weight of the ten of 440 bolls is 51·76428 tons.

The ten is also defined by weight as to consist of 18½ Newcastle chaldrons of 53 cwt. In this case the weight of the ten is 48·58333 cwt. but this not a ten of 440 bolls.

In some leases the ten is fixed at 50 tons.

TENTALE.—The rent paid to the lessor for a ten of coals. (See *Rent*.)

THILL.—The floor of a seam of coal.

THRUST.—(See *Crush*.)

THUD.—A dull and heavy report made by the rending of the strata far overhead when the coal has been extracted.

TIE BAND.—"A piece of rope or spunyarn used in securing long timber or rails when being sent down in the cage." (*Nicholson*.)

TOKEN.—(See *Average Weight*.)

TOOM.—Empty.

TOP.—(See *Show*.)

TRAIL JUD.—In driving a wide board to drive forward 3 or 4 yards narrow, and then take off a jud sideways, to make the board the proper width.

TRAM.—A wooden carriage, upon which the corves were conveyed along a tramway. Since the substitution of tubs, the trams and tubs are attached together. A tram with 4 or more upright arms of iron used for conveying rails, props, &c., is called a horny tram.

TRAM PLATE.—An iron or metal rail of the section L and weighing about 4 lbs. to the foot, with which the way for the passage of carriages moving on tram or edged wheels, is laid.

TRAP.—The part of a skreen, near to the upper end, shut off by a door worked by a handle by the skreenman, by which the coals from the last tub teemed on the skreen are prevented from passing down until the previous tub has been disposed of, and by which door, in proportion as it is raised, the skreenman can control the rush of the coals down the skreen. Also whin, or basalt of whin dykes, called also trap dykes. Also an accident to which, without proper precaution, putters are liable, when from an obstruction in front, the back top edge of the tub, upon which the fingers are usually placed, cants against the top in a low seam. A couple of hand-holes cut in the ends of the tubs, or cut down below the top edge is an easy remedy.

TRAP-DOOR.—(See *Door.*)

TRAPPER.—A little boy whose employment consists in opening and shutting a trap-door when required: his wages are 9d. or 10d. per day of 12 hours (1849). At present 1s. to 1s. 2d. per day of 8 hours.

TRIANGLES.—(See *Bore.*)

TRIM.—When coals from the waggons are dropped or spouted into the hold of a vessel they produce a conical heap which, unless provided against, would soon block up the hatchway. To prevent this, sheets of iron are laid upon the cone as it rises which cause the coals to slide off in all directions; these are placed by a set of men, called trimmers, who with shovels and rakes still further distribute the coal, or trim the cargo.

TRIMMERS.—(See *Trim.*)

TROD.—The diameter of a flanched wheel, not including the flanch.

TROUBLE.—(See *Hitch, Fault, &c.*)

TUB.—An open topped box of wood or iron, attached to a tram, and used in conveying coals from the working places to the surface.

TUBBING.—A casing put into a pit to keep back water. It was formerly put in with planks, properly dressed at the joints to the sweep of the pit, and kept in their places by being spiked to cribs behind them. Tubbing was also constructed of cribs of oak, built one upon another to the required height, and afterwards wedged; this formed an excellent but expensive tub. At present, tubbing is put in in metal segments. The commencement is made by laying a metal or oak wedging crib at the first good foundation below the feeder of water to be tubbed back, and then setting on the segments, backing the tubbing firmly with soil all the way up so far as it is required to be put in. Half inch sheathing of American fir should be put in at both ends and bottom of each segment, and baff ends and spares driven in behind so as to set the tubbing true to the centre line of the pit. The segments are usually from $1\frac{1}{2}$ to 2 feet high, and about 4 feet long, according to the size of the pit, so that a certain number of segments may form the pit. When the tubbing is all built up, and made secure at the top so that it will not rise with wedging, the joints are wedged with memel wedges, as long as they can be driven in at the joints, the whole being gone twice or thrice over.

TUBE, CUBE, CUPOLA.—(See *Cube.*)

TUP.—In former days there used to be a fortnight's holiday at the end of the year, when stock used to be taken and no coals drawn. It was the custom to cover with lighted candles the last corf of coals sent to bank, which was called "sending away the tup." The tup's horn, which used to be sent up with every twentieth corf, also accompanied the illuminated corf.

TRYING THE CANDLE.—(See *Show.*)

UNDER-CAST, UNDER-GATE.—(See *Crossing.*)

UNDER-LEVEL DRIFT.—(See *Standage.*)

UNDER-VIEWER.—The responsible manager of a colliery in the absence of the viewer.

UP-CAST.—A rise hitch: the shaft up which the air returns from the workings to the surface.

UP-THROW.—A rise hitch, smaller than an up-cast.

V-BOB.—A half beam of the form of a letter V. It is placed horizontally in a chamber made for the purpose in a pumping shaft. Its main gudgeon is placed at the point of the V, and inner end of the chamber, and works in a fixed carriage. The other end of the V-bob projects into the pit, from the gudgeon at the lower end of which the spears are hung. The gudgeon in the upper limb, which is a little shorter, is connected by a spear passing through a diagonal staple under the main engine-house, with a gudgeon in the main beam, at a point between the cylinder and the main beam pillar. This arrangement is not adopted in modern practice.

VIEWER.—The manager of a colliery; one who has the charge of all underground, and generally of all surface, arrangements.

WAGGON WAY.—Railway, rolleyway.

WALL.—The holing or communication at the end of a pillar between two boards; several walls in a line form a headways course.

WAILERS.—Boys employed in waggons, to pick out any stones or pyrites which have escaped the observation of the skreenmen.

WASH.—An ancient river bed, since silted up, and very difficult to sink through. Washes are sometimes of great depth, as in the valley of the Team, at Marley Hill, and elsewhere.

WASTE.—The old workings and airways.

WASTEMEN.—Generally old men, who are employed in building pillars for the support of the roof in the waste, and in keeping the airways open and in good order. Their wages are about 2s. 4d. per day. A master wasteman has (under the viewer or underviewer) the charge of the waste, and should be a steady and careful man, and have some skill in ventilation. His wages are about 21s. per week (1849.)

WATER-BLAST.—A sudden eruption of compressed gas from the rise workings of a colliery in which all communications between such workings and the external atmosphere have been cut off by water. The continued issue of gas eventually overcoming the pressure of the water, forces its way out and produces the blast.

WATERFALL.—A circulation of air through a mine produced by allowing water to fall down one of the shafts.

WAY.—A working district underground.

WAYLEAVE RENT.—(See *Rent.*)

WEDGE.—For wedging tubbing, &c., made from Memel plank, 4½ inches long, 1½ inch broad, and ½ inch thick at the top, tapered a little at the sides towards the thin end. For wedging down coal juds or stone, made of iron or steel 6 or 8 inches long, flattened towards and pointed at the end.

WEDGING CRIB.—(See *Tubbing.*)

WEIZE.—" A flat iron ring covered with flannel for making pipe joints watertight. Rings of spunyarn, India rubber or lead are also used for the same purpose." (*Nicholson.*) The flannel wrapped round the iron should be well saturated with Stockholm tar; and when made of lead, it should be carefully caulked with a flat edged chisel.

WET SPEARS.—(See *Spears.*)

WHIN.—Basalt, trap.

WHIN DYKE.—(See *Dyke.*)

WHOLE COAL — A district of coal entirely intact.

WIDE BOARD.—(See *Board.*)

WIMBLE.—(See *Bore.*)

WINDBORE.—The bottom pump in a set. (See *Snoreholes.*)

WINNING.—A pillar of coal with its board; also a recovery of coal, by sinking, or drifting in coal or stone.

WIRE-DRAWN.—An engine is wire-drawn when there are not a sufficient number of holes in the wind-bore left open for waterway.

WORKING.—The crackling of roof stone previous to falling.

WORKING BARREL.—The portion of a pump in which the bucket works (see *Lifting Set*). An easy rule for calculating the quantity of water drawn at a single stroke in a working barrel of a given diameter, is as follows :—Square the diameter in inches, and divide by 10 for the gallons in a 3 feet stroke.

WORKINGS.—The excavations of a colliery.

Y-PIECE.—Framed timber hung on to the outer end of the beam of a pumping engine to which the spears are attached.

YARD PRICE.—The price per yard paid for narrow working.

YARD WORK.—(See *Narrow Work*.)

YOKING.—When two sets of waggons approaching each other on the same line, come into collision.

THE END.

www.ingramcontent.com/pod-product-compliance
Lightning Source LLC
Chambersburg PA
CBHW020900160426
43192CB00007B/1011